Other books by the same author published by Lycabettus Press

St. John of Patmos and the Seven Churches of the Apocalypse

St. Paul in Ephesus and the Cities of Galatia and Cyprus

ST. PAUL IN GREECE

Otto F.A. Meinardus

Lycabettus Press

ISBN 960-7269-17-9

Published by
Lycabettus Press
P. O. Box 17091
Athens 10024
Greece

Fax: (30 1) 671 0666
Telephone: (30 1) 674 1788
e-mail: jchapple@ath.forthnet.gr

First edition, 1972. Second edition, 1973. Third edition, 1977. Fourth edition, 1984. Fifth edition, 1989. Sixth edition, 1992; second printing, 1994; third printing, 1995; fourth printing, 1997.

Printed in Greece by
Corfu
Smolenski 9
Athens 11472

CONTENTS

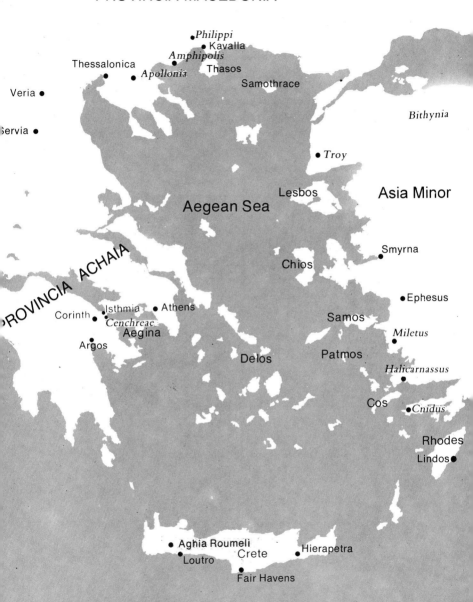

SUGGESTED CHRONOLOGY

St. Paul made three missionary journeys and a final journey to Rome. The first missionary journey was to Cyprus and Asia Minor. The second and the third missionary journeys were to Asia Minor and Greece. The fourth and final journey was from Palestine to Rome.

Fall of 48	Beginning of second missionary journey, from Antioch to Derbe, Lystra, Iconium, Phrygia, and Troy.
Spring of 49	Neapolis (Kavalla), Philippi, Thessalonica, Veria, and Athens.
Spring of 50	Arrival in Corinth.
Summer of 51	Accusation before Gallio, the proconsul in Corinth.
Fall of 51	Departure from Corinth. Return to Antioch via Ephesus, Caesarea, and Jerusalem.
Spring of 53	Beginning of third missionary journey. Visits in Phrygia and Galatia.
Fall of 54	Journey to Ephesus where he stayed for approximately two and one half years, during which he made a brief visit to the church in Corinth.
Summer of 57	Macedonia.
Winter 57-58	Corinth, for three months.
Spring of 58	Return through Macedonia to Caesarea.
Fall of 61	Crete.

PREFACE

One more book on the Apostle Paul? Haven't scholars, historians and theologians written enough about the life, the travels and the theology of this man? Certainly, a great deal has been published about him if one considers only the 84 books on St. Paul listed in the *Subject Guide to Books in Print 1970,* or the 2,987 articles entered in the *Index to Periodical Literature on the Apostle Paul.* By far the majority of these books and articles on St. Paul, however, are unavailable to the tourist interested in retracing the steps of the Apostle in Greece unless he is determined to research in the famous Gennadion Library on the southern slopes of Lycabettus in Athens. Otherwise the inquisitive visitor will find it virtually impossible to obtain much information about the Apostle's ministry in Greece. While serving as pastor of St. Andrew's American Church in Athens during the past few years, I have seen many visitors go out of their way for guidance and information about the actual places associated with the spread of the Gospel in Greece. The following pages are written in response to this interest, in the hope that they will help the historically oriented and religiously motivated tourist find his visit to some of the ancient biblical sites a more meaningful encounter with the past.

At the very outset of these pages we want to acknowledge the widespread and popular dispute about the relationship of the message of Jesus to that of St. Paul. Neither the person nor the message of the Apostle need any apology, but there are many sincere Christians who hesitate to get too deeply involved with the life and writing of the missionary Apostle. Endorsing the 19th century slogan of liberal Protestantism, "Back to Jesus," many Christians feel that they can rely exclusively on the sayings and the portrait of the "historical Jesus" as the norm for their Christian life and, therefore, react negatively to the "religion about Jesus" as spelled out by St. Paul. Others accuse him for having perverted the simplicity of Jesus' message by unnecessarily shrouding it in theological and christological concepts. No matter where we turn, there are many people who say "no" to St. Paul while at the same time affirming a strong "yes" for Jesus. The debate about the great missionary and theologian of the early Church and his message is, of course, as old as the Christian Church. Even during his lifetime his opponents regarded him as an illegitimate apostle and an adulterator of the Christian Gospel, and the fathers of the early Church were inconsistent in their judgment. The author of Pseudo-Clement, for example, compared him with Simon Magus, the heresiarch par excellence, while others gave him the highest consideration and quoted his letters at length in their own writings.

Whether or not the Apostle was familiar with the message preached by Jesus is a question to which historians and theologians have given different answers, although it is certain that none of the Gospels in the form as they appear in the New Testament were known to him. St. Paul stressed a different aspect. Jesus proclaimed the messages of the Fatherhood and the Kingdom of God. The Apostle emphasized the Cross and the Resurrection of Jesus as the Christ.

Whatever the differences, St. Paul's travels and ministry are tremendously meaningful, especially because of the intensely situational character of his preaching. If anyone ever looked at the world realistically, it was the Apostle Paul; if anyone ever recognized the need for a revolutionary faith and ethic, again, it was the Apostle Paul. As are a few Christians in the 20th century, he was able to relate the liberating power of the Gospel to concrete situations, and this is especially evident in his writings to the churches in Greece. St. Paul wrote in response to immediate problems in the lives of people he knew, and he could never have dreamt that his explicitly situational correspondence would ever be collected and then accepted as a norm for Christian theology and ethics. As a messenger of the power of God unto salvation, St. Paul ought to be regarded as a prototype rather than as an example to be followed blindly. He served as mouthpiece of the very God Who revealed Himself in Jesus as the Christ, and as such the Apostle's message is invaluable to our understanding of the Christian Gospel. That there are contradictions or various degrees of emphasis in his statements should only enhance him to us for, though always conscious of his divine mission, he remained a man of flesh and blood. He was a theologian, not a systematician, and to press his statements into a preconceived dogmatic mold is methodologically illegitimate and robs him and his writings of their liberating power.

As for source material, we are in the fortunate position of knowing more about St. Paul than about any other person of the early Church. Our knowledge about most of the Holy Apostles is very limited, and many of the legends and traditions related about them developed long after they lived. Even with respect to the person of Our Lord Jesus Christ, the central theme of the Apostle's message to the churches in Greece, the historian is in a much more difficult situation, for whatever we know about Jesus must be seen and evaluated through the eyes of the fellowship of believers. The Gospel narratives, therefore, are statements of confessions of faith of the post-resurrection Church rather than biographical descriptions of what has been called the "historical Jesus." We possess no evidence, for instance, that Our Lord ever wrote a letter, not to mention a book. In contrast, St. Paul's personality and a great deal of other information pertaining to the Apostle's life are reflected in the New Testament epistular literature, of which thirteen documents claim his authorship.

This brief preface is not the place to discuss the thorny

and certainly still undecided issues with respect to the authenticity of the various letters which carry the name of the Apostle. At the same time, we must recognize that the majority of these letters are invaluable for any kind of reconstruction of the Apostle's ministry. The letters, especially those addressed to the churches in Greece (the letters to the Thessalonians, Corinthians, and Philippians), are primary sources for our study. These letters, addressed to his newly founded communities on the European mainland, were unquestionably written by St. Paul. Furthermore, in evaluating this material it is important for us to remember that, for example, the First Letter of Paul to the Thessalonians constitutes the very beginning of Christian literature. It was written about the middle of the first century, only twenty years after the death and resurrection of Our Lord. For that matter, all the letters with which we are concerned in this particular essay date to the fifties of the first century. They were written at least a decade prior to the writing of the oldest Gospel, the Gospel of St. Mark.

The second New Testament source relevant to our study is the Acts of the Apostles, in which St. Luke sketched the beginnings of Christianity, especially Christianity in Greece. The narrative begins with a description of the Jerusalem Church and culminates in Rome, where the Christian faith, mysteriously, has already been established. More than half of this book centers around the missionary activities of the Apostle Paul. Many scholars have considered the Acts as their principal source for their understanding of the Apostle's ministry. This is unfortunate because the Acts of the Apostles was written at a much later time, when the Christian Church was fairly well established in the eastern Mediterranean world. It is a pity that St. Luke was unacquainted with the Pauline letters, since they would, of course, have been of great value to him when writing about the life and work of St. Paul. St. Luke, furthermore, did not merely repeat what he had heard or read from the several sources at his disposal, but used his material to instruct his readers. He portrayed St. Paul not only as having died, but as already having become a hallowed memory. In the Acts, St. Paul is no longer a man grappling with difficulties as he is in his letters; he has become a heroic figure towering above priests, officers, governors, and kings.

A comparison of the image which St. Paul portrays of himself in his own writings with that presented to us almost fifty years later in the Acts of the Apostles, reveals differences which force us to rely on St. Paul's own letters rather than categorically follow the Lukan version of the Acts. A list of the numerous discrepancies between these two sources can be found easily in any reputable study of the Apostle. In case of conflicting statements, we give preference to the personal testimony of the Apostle.

Despite its limitations, the narrative of the Acts of the Apostles gives us a welcome guideline to the itinerary of the Apostle's travels in Greece. All quotations from the Holy Scriptures are from the Revised Standard Version of the Bible, copyrighted in 1946 and 1952 by the Division of Christian Education of the National Council of Churches of Christ in the U.S.A., and are used by permission. For many helpful and invaluable suggestions, I should like to thank my colleagues of the American School of Classical Studies in Athens and, finally, I must express my sincere gratitude to my secretary, Mrs. Sophia Hanazoglu, for preparing the manuscript for the press.

Otto F.A. Meinardus

1972, Athens, Greece

St. Paul from a 6th century terracotta

Courtesy of the Benaki Museum, Athens.

INTRODUCTION

A Biographical Note

St. Paul, the great Apostle to the Gentiles, holds a place in the Church of Jesus Christ second only to that of the Founder. Although we are ignorant as to the exact date of his birth, we may assume that he was born around the beginning of the Christian era in Tarsus, one of the principal cities of the Roman province of Cilicia, in southern Asia Minor. Firstly, his birth as a free citizen in a Roman province made him a Roman citizen (Acts 22:28). He had, unquestionably, in addition to his name Paul, another Roman name which, however, has remained unrecorded. Secondly, he held full rights as a citizen of his native city, of which he was proud (Acts 21:39). Thirdly, he was "a Hebrew, born of Hebrews," to strict Jewish parents. He was a Jew as much as he was a Tarsian and a Roman, and this three-fold identity has helped to make him such a controversial person. To the Hebrews in the diaspora he emphasized his Jewish origin and character; with the Greeks he conversed in their native tongue; with the Roman authorities he stressed his claims as a Roman citizen.

From his statements in his letters we understand that he was brought up as a strict Jew; not as a Sadducee, but rather as a Pharisee. "Are they Hebrews? So am I. Are they Israelites? So am I. Are they descendants of Abraham? So am I " (II Cor. 11:22). "Circumcised on the eighth day, of the people of Israel, of the tribe of Benjamin, a Hebrew born of Hebrews; As to the law a Pharisee" (Phil. 3:5). His Jewish name, Saul, had been bestowed upon him in memory of the first king of the Jewish nation.

Nonetheless, there were strong Hellenistic influences upon his personality. The language of his childhood was Greek, as was the language in which all his letters were written. He had learned Hebrew and, while studying under Gamaliel at Jerusalem (Acts 22:3) he must have acquired a thorough knowledge of that language. The version of the Old Testament, however, with which he was most familiar was the Greek translation known as the Septuagint, for whenever he quoted from the Old Testament he did so from that version. The readiness with which he expressed himself in Greek shows a command of the language he could hardly have attained had it not been the familiar speech of his youth.

About his family we know next to nothing. He merely alluded to his father. We know that his sister had a son (Acts 23:16), and he referred to some distant relatives (Rom. 16:7,11, 21). He made no mention whatsoever of his mother.

We do not know how old Saul was when he moved from Tarsus to Jerusalem, where he encountered the strange new sectarian movement of Christians. It is at this point that the Acts of the Apostles begins the story of his persecutions of the people of the new faith, his conversion on the Damascus Road, and his heroic service for his newly discovered Lord. He ceased to be Saul, the Jewish rabbi, perhaps even a member of the Sanhedrin, and became Paul the Apostle, the chief figure in the early years of the Christian Church.

The Call to Macedonia

> Passing by Mysia, they went down to Troas. And a vision appeared to Paul in the night: a man of Macedonia was standing beseeching him and saying, "Come over to Macedonia and help us." And when he had seen the vision, immediately we sought to go on into Macedonia, concluding that God had called us to preach the gospel to them.
>
> Acts 16:8-10

Among the "abundance of revelations" (II Cor. 12:7) which was given to St. Paul, two extraordinary and intensely personal experiences determined the course of the Apostle's life. The best known is the Apostle's confrontation with the Risen Christ on the Damascus Road, which converted him to the Christian faith and empowered him to preach the newly discovered truth to Jews and Gentiles alike. For our purpose, however, St. Paul's vision in the ancient city of Troy is not less significant. His mission to the peoples in Greece received its inspiration from this particular call, which occurred during St. Paul's second missionary journey in the autumn of the year 48, while the Apostle, together with Silas and his newly won companion Timothy, were passing through Phrygia and Galatia on their way to Troy.

Three distinct factors led to St. Paul's mission in Europe. The narrator of the Acts informs us that the Holy Spirit prevented them from declaring the message of Christ in the province of Asia; that the Spirit of Jesus would not allow them to enter Bithynia, and that, finally, a vision directed St. Paul to Macedonia. Whether our three missionaries were prevented from preaching the Gospel in western Anatolia because of St. John's missionary activities there is a matter of pure conjecture.

The Apostle could hardly have been aware that he was standing on top of nine main layers corresponding to the nine groups of successive settlements which, since the excavations by Heinrich Schliemann (1872-1874) and Wilhelm Dörpfeld (1891-1894) and more recently by the archaeologists of the University of Cincinnati, have been brought to light. Here, on the site of Homeric fame, Lysimachus, a lieutenant of Alexander the Great, rebuilt the town, which he named Alexandria Troas in honor of his master, another "man of Macedonia." Over the centuries, kings and princes had come to Troy. Xerxes had passed by this city on his campaign to conquer Greece and, in 334, Alexander visited this venerable site and sacrificed to the Ilian Athena, paying homage at the tomb of Achilles and making his offerings to the great Homeric dead. Julius Caesar was here after the battle of Pharsalia. In fact, Alexandria Troas enjoyed the legacy of the city of Priam, but it also pointed to another city, which for centuries to come was to be the center of the empire, Constantinople. For not only did Caesar turn his eyes to Troy as a possibility for his capital, Constantine the Great, before finally selecting Byzantium, had entertained the idea of erecting the seat of his empire on this historic site. It is no mere coincidence, therefore, that the Ottoman Turks referred to the ruins of Troy as Eski-Stamboul or Old Constantinople. The Emperor Augustus had bestowed upon Troy not only the privileges of a Roman colony, but also granted to her the *ius Italicum,* which meant that the land enjoyed the same tax exemptions as the land in Italy. When St. Paul, in the company of Silas and Timothy, reached Troy, many of the Roman installations planned for this site had not been built, and the Roman aqueduct as well as the Roman walls should be assigned to a later period.

For the student of the Holy Scriptures, St. Paul's stay in Troy and his meeting with the "man of Macedonia" are particularly interesting because at this point in the Acts of the Apostles the person of the narrative suddenly changes. As soon as the Apostle had seen his vision, "we" then made every effort to get on to Macedonia. The introduction of the first person plural was certainly intentional, and the reader must notice that the author of this particular episode was an eye-witness to the events he recorded. Modern scholarship refers to those portions of the Acts of the Apostles which use the first person plural as the "we-sections" (Acts 16:10-18; 20:5-16; 21:1-18; 27:1-28:16). They were written, undoubtedly, by a companion of St. Paul.

Who was this "man of Macedonia" appearing in the vision in Troy? The Apostle, apparently, did not only listen to a voice as he did during his experience on the Damascus Road. He saw a man and he recognized him as a Macedonian by sight, although in the days of St. Paul there were no apparent distinctions in dress between the inhabitants of the eastern and western shores of the Aegean Sea. It seems likely, therefore, that St. Paul had some prior acquaintance with this person who appeared to him in a dream in Troy. William M. Ramsay and others have suggested that perhaps this person was St. Luke, the "beloved physician" (Col. 4:14). St. Paul may have met the physician even in Antioch, which tradition has assigned as the birthplace of St. Luke. Moreover, the detailed information in the Acts concerning the spreading of the Gospel in Antioch implies the physician's connection with that church. His name, a familiarization of Lucanus or Lucius, indicates that he may have been the son of a Greek freedman of some Roman family, and since Julius Caesar had bestowed Roman citizenship upon all physicians in Rome, St. Luke may well have enjoyed this status. This is purely hypothetical, but it seems likely that St. Luke may have practiced medicine in Philippi and, either upon hearing of the Apostle's arrival in Troy or by arrangement, met St. Paul in the ancient Homeric city. We see no reason, therefore, why this certain "man of Macedonia" could not have been the third Evangelist, who was living in the Roman colony of Philippi upon which he looked as his city.

Arrival

Setting sail therefore from Troas, we made a direct voyage to Samothrace, and the following day to Neapolis.

Acts 16:11

Setting sail from Troy, they (Sts. Paul, Silas, Timothy, and Luke), ran a straight course to Samothrace. To the west they must have seen the summit of Mount Athos, which on clear days can be seen even from the Asiatic coastline. The weather conditions were in the sailors' favor, for the trip from Troy to Neapolis took only two days. On a later occasion, when St. Paul returned from his third missionary journey, it took him five days to sail the other direction, from Neapolis to Troy (Acts 20:6). The text informs us that on this journey they sailed before the wind, so we may assume that the wind blew from the south, which would explain their anchoring for the night in Samothrace. As W.J. Conybeare wrote, "What Mount Athos is to the Christian of the Levant, the peak of Samothrace was in the days of heathenism to his Greek ancestors in the same seas." If St. Paul had stayed in Samothrace for some time, he undoubtedly would have visited the sanctuary of the great gods, but we have no reason to suppose that he even landed on the island. The following day the travelers continued their voyage and, after passing the island of Thasos, they landed on the coast of Thrace, in Neapolis, the port of Philippi. This landing was one of the great moments in the history of Christianity; the definitive step of its progress from

5

the East to the West. Neither St. Paul nor St. Luke, however, could have been aware of this geographical distinction. For them the journey from Troy to Neapolis was only a matter of sailing from one Roman province to another, from Asia to Macedonia.

As in the case of so many ancient cities, the name of the port where they landed has changed with the passage of time. Known

First-century ships in the Roman harbor of Ostia as depicted on a sestertius of the emperor Nero (54-68 A.D.)

Kavalla: View of the waterfront

by the ancient Greeks as Neapolis, in Byzantine days it was called Christopolis when it became a suffragan bishopric of Philippi, undoubtedly in commemoration of St. Paul's visit. In the Middle Ages the Franks called it Christople. The Ottomans gave it the name Cavallo, a vulgarization of the Latin word meaning "horse," because it was used as an important station in the Ottoman postal service. It was the birthplace of Muhammad Ali, the ruler of Egypt from 1805 until 1848.

Kavalla, as the town came to be known, was part of the Ottoman Empire from 1387 until after the Balkan War of 1912-1913 when it was incorporated into Greece. During the First World War the town was occupied by the Bulgarians, but it was returned to Greece in 1918. In 1941 Kavalla was occupied again by the Bulgarians after the German invasion of Greece during the Second World War, but it was returned to Greece in 1944. Today Kavalla is Greece's principal exporting center for Macedonian tobacco.

The Church of St. Paul, which commemorates the Apostle's arrival in Neapolis, was built in 1928. H.V. Morton refers to a Church of St. Nicholas which, prior to the Turkish occupation of the city, was supposed to have been known as the Church of St. Paul. There is, however, no historical evidence for this tradition. During the Ottoman period the building in question was converted into a mosque, and it was rebuilt only in 1930. Behind the church is what appears to be the remains of a column drum imbedded in the sidewalk, which some people consider to mark the spot where St. Paul stepped ashore.

MACEDONIA

Philippi

PREACHING

> And from there [we went]to Philippi, which is the leading ci-
> ty of the district of Macedonia, and a Roman colony. We re-
> mained in this city some days; and on the sabbath day we
> went outside the gate to the riverside, where we supposed
> there was a place of prayer; and we sat down and spoke to
> the women who had come together. One who heard us was
> a woman named Lydia, from the city of Thyatira, a seller of
> purple goods, who was a worshiper of God. The Lord open-
> ed her heart to give heed to what was said by Paul. And
> when she was baptized, with her household, she besought us,
> saying, "If you have judged me to be faithful to the Lord,
> come to my house and stay." And she prevailed upon us. As
> we were going to the place of prayer, we were met by a slave
> girl who had a spirit of divination and brought her owners
> much gain by soothsaying. She followed Paul and us, crying,
> "These men are servants of the Most High God, who pro-
> claim to you the way of salvation." And this she did for
> many days. But Paul was annoyed, and turned and said to
> the spirit, "I charge you in the name of Jesus Christ to come
> out of her." And it came out that very hour.
>
> Acts 16:12-18

From Neapolis the missionaries went to Philippi, which was
a Roman garrison town and the chief city in the province of Macedonia. Following the main road, part of the Via Egnatia which
connected the harbor with Philippi, the Apostle and his associates
must have seen the Pangaeus mountain range, famous in antiquity
for its gold mines, before descending to the fertile plain between Mts. Haemus and Pangaeus. The ruins of Philippi extend
over a large area and may today conveniently be reached by

taking the road from Kavalla to Drama. After eight miles the ruins of the 2nd century forum appear on the left some fifteen feet below the present ground level. On the right are the remains of Basilica A and, further on, the ancient theater. The city was founded by Philip II of Macedonia in the 4th century B.C., but it gained fame only later on account of the historic battle which ended the Roman Republic. Here the legions commanded by Caesar's assassins, Brutus and Cassius, were defeated by the troops of Octavius and Antony. The assassins committed suicide after the battle, and the victors granted the city the privilege of a Roman colony, thereby elevating it to the position of a border garrison. As a Roman garrison town, Philippi was a miniature of Rome. Its language was Latin and its law was Roman, and the money of the colony bore Latin inscriptions. Its full name was Colonia Augusta Julia Philippensis.

A colony like Philippi was inhabited by two types of Roman citizens. The first were genuine Italians who had been commissioned to live in a colony; the second were what might be called "political proselytes." Both St. Paul and Silas belonged to this second category, which entitled them to the same rights as those possessed by Romans of Roman stock: for example, exemption from scourging, freedom from arrest except in extreme cases, and the right to appeal to the emperor; privileges of which St. Paul was much aware when he was later arrested in Jerusalem. We know very little about the indigenous Macedonian population in this city. The number of Jews in Philippi must have been very small, for instead of a synagogue they maintained only a proseuche, a temporary place of prayer outside the city gate. This proseuche was near the river so that the necessary ablutions connected with their worship could easily be performed. It seems plausible to seek the motive for these ablutions in the ritual uncleanness of the land of the Gentiles, especially in view of the following passage of the Midrash:

> And although, for the merit of the Fathers, He spake unto them (the Prophets) outside the land, yet did He only speak unto them in a clean place, by water, as it is written, "and I was by the stream of Ulai" (Dan. 8:2), or "as I was by the river, which is Tigris" (Dan. 10:4).

But before we shall discuss the Apostle's missionary activities in Philippi and the detailed descriptions of the course of events, we must recognize the importance which both the Apostle and the narrator attributed to the establishment of the first congregation on European soil. If we compare, for example, the twenty-eight verses in which St. Luke accounts for the Apostle's ministry in Philippi with the nine verses devoted to St. Paul's stay in Thessalonica or even the five verses which speak of his preaching in Veria, we notice that the Apostle's ministry to the Philippians must have been considered a strategic success not only for St. Paul and St. Luke, but also for the early Church, which retained and cherished this apostolic experience. The lengthy description of the ministry in Philippi can be explained by attributing to the narrator some extraordinary interest in the city. We have already suggested that it may have been his second home. The statement in Acts 16:12 that "we remained in this city some days" implies a short stay, but other indications, such as the incident with the ventriloquist who followed the Apostle "for many days" (Acts 16:18) point to a longer residence. In contrast to the popular view of a brief Philippian ministry, the numerous episodes recorded in connection with the Apostle's stay in Philippi suggest a longer stay, perhaps even for several weeks.

St. Paul won his first European convert, a woman, in Philippi. Modern feminists are often quite critical of St. Paul who, after all, wrote, "Neither was man created for woman, but woman for man" (I Cor. 11:9), "The women should keep silence in the churches (I Cor. 14:34), and "Wives, be subject to your husbands" (Col. 3:18). Nonetheless, women played a significant role in the early Church and, although no women were of the Twelve, women were often "with" them. They were, moreover, singled out for special mention as a group standing within sight of the Cross of Calvary (Luke 23:49, 55). Philip, one of the first seven deacons in Caesarea, Palestine, was the father of four virgins who prophesied (Acts 21:8, 9). To the south, along the Mediterranean coast at Joppa, St. Peter found the congregation centered upon "a disciple named Tabitha....She was full of good works and acts of charity" (Acts 9:36). In Greece, women played a dominant role in the life of the early Pauline congregations. One of the hearers

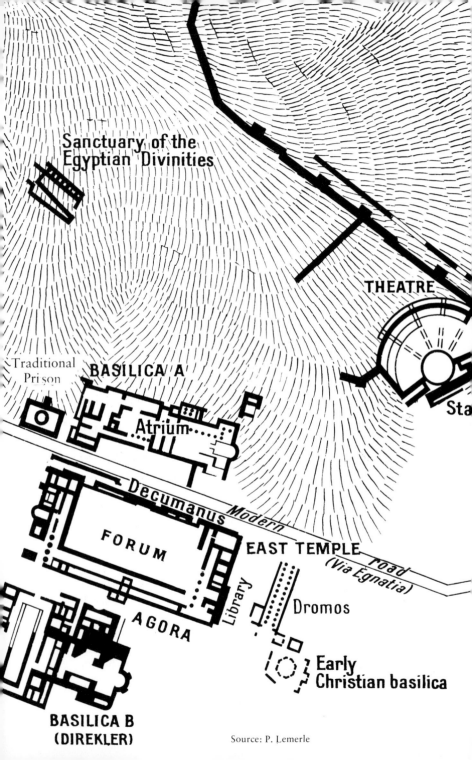

Sanctuary of the
Egyptian Divinities

THEATRE

Traditional
Prison

BASILICA A

Atrium

Sta

Decumanus

Modern

FORUM

EAST TEMPLE

road

(Via Egnatia)

Library

Dromos

AGORA

Early
Christian basilica

BASILICA B
(DIREKLER)

Source: P. Lemerle

in Philippi was a woman named Lydia who, although already a believer in God, accepted the Apostle's words and was baptized with all her household (Acts 16:14,15). In Thessalonica the missionaries converted "a great many of the devout Greeks and not a few of the leading women" (Acts 17:4). Similarly, in Veria "Many of them therefore, believed, with not a few of Greek women of high standing as well as men" (Acts 17:12). In Athens, one of the two persons mentioned by name as having accepted the Gospel was a woman named Damaris (Acts 17:34). St. Paul included eight women in the list of twenty-six people ending the Letter to the Romans, and he mentioned six of these eight with distinction. About the wife of Aquila, Priscilla, who was such a faithful helper of the Apostle in Corinth and later in Ephesus, we shall comment later. This is sufficient evidence that women played an important role in the life of the early Church and that St. Paul, so often misunderstood for his anti-feminine remarks, relied heavily upon the women in his new congregations in Greece.

St. Paul's first European convert, Lydia of the town of Thyatira in the province of Lydia, Asia Minor, came to Philippi because she was a dealer in purple dyed cloth, a business which had flourished in her native province from ancient days. Thyatira today is the Turkish town of Akhisar, well known as a center for carpet making. Since Lydia was a householder and her husband is not mentioned, we assume that she was a widow. The reference to her as a believer in God suggests that she may have accepted the Jewish faith in Thyatira where a Jewish colony existed. St. John, the Seer of Patmos, addressed one of his seven letters to the church of Thyatira, in which we are informed of the prevalent religious syncretism in this city. Lydia was not the only representative of her trade in Philippi. In 1872 Professor Mertzides discovered in Philippi the following text in Greek inscribed on a piece of white marble: "The city honored from among the purple-dyers, an outstanding citizen, Antiochus the

Philippi: Plan of the ancient city

son of Lykus, a native of Thyatira, as a benefactor." The marble with this inscription, which has unfortunately disappeared, indicates that the purple-dyers of Thyatira may have worked in Philippi as a guild and that their profession was held in high esteem.

Lydia heard the Apostle's message and was convinced that Jesus is the Christ. She made a profession of faith, and she and her household were baptized. The place of the baptism was probably the banks of the Gaggitas River, which, in the decisive battle between the forces of Antony and Octavian and those of Brutus and Cassius, had been polluted by the blood of the contending armies. Today, the crystal clear stream flows through tobacco fields. After her baptism Lydia invited the Apostle to her house, asking him to stay there. This type of Christian hospitality became an important part of the apostolic message: "Do not neglect to show hospitality to strangers, for thereby some have entertained angels unawares" (Heb. 13:2). Moreover, we see here the beginnings of the Christian family religion, which is repeatedly referred to by St. Paul in his letters, *e.g.* the household of Stephanas (I Cor. 1:16; 16:5), or the church in the house of Priscilla and Aquila (Rom. 16:5). According to a local tradition, Lydia's house was in the village which has adopted her name, several hundred feet beyond the ruins of Philippi. Some people even feel that the Hotel Lidia may have been built on the site of the house where the Apostle stayed. A chapel commemorating Lydia's baptism has been built nearby.

For a while the young church in Philippi enjoyed peace. Every Sabbath the little congregation went out of the city gate to the riverside, where they assembled for worship. One day as they proceeded to their place of prayer, a young slave girl possessed of a Spirit Python met them. The Greeks believed that oracular power was a gift bestowed by Apollo, who was considered the god of pythonic spirits. Such prophetesses, like the Pythones and Eurycleidai, however, were the lowest members of the profession, which was headed by the Pythia of the Delphic oracle. This particular girl had brought her owners a great deal of profit and, sensing a threat to her profession, she followed St. Paul and the small Christian congregation crying out for all to hear, "These men are servants of the Most High God, who proclaim to you the way of salvation " (Acts 16:17). She did this for many days until the Apostle, losing patience, turned around to her and exorcised the spirit, which left her immediately, in the name of Jesus. The reaction to St. Paul's first exorcism on European soil was immediate. The slave girl lost her ability to speak as she had done. Her power and influence over people vanished and the comfortable income she had earned for her masters was lost. Therefore, they sought revenge.

IMPRISONMENT

> But when her owners saw that their hope of gain was gone, they seized Paul and Silas and dragged them into the market place before the rulers; and when they had brought them to the magistrates they said, "These men are Jews and they are disturbing our city. They advocate customs which it is not lawful for us Romans to accept or practice." The crowd joined in attacking them; and the magistrates tore the garments off them and gave orders to beat them with rods. And when they had inflicted many blows upon them, they threw them into prison, charging the jailer to keep them safely. Having received this charge, he put them into the inner prison and fastened their feet in the stocks.
>
> Acts 16:19-24

The masters of the slave girl were unable to accuse the Apostle for his practice of exorcism, for Roman law had no clause concerning property depreciated by that practice. Instead they based their charge on political foundations; causing civic disturbance and introducing new religious observances. The first accusation was false, for there is no evidence that the peace of the city was in any way threatened by the Christian missionaries. The other charge, however, was considerably weightier, for Roman law did prohibit the introduction of foreign religions. The fact that they were Jews was included in the accusation. The Jews had been expelled from Rome at approximately the same time, between January 49 and January 50, and a border colony like Philippi might well have emulated the attitude of the capital. In this context it is interesting to note that, contrary to the usual course of events as described by St. Luke, it was not the Jews who stirred up trouble in Philippi as, for example, they did in Pisidian Antioch, Lystra, and later in Thessalonica and Corinth, but it was the Romans who denounced both St. Paul and Silas.

The affairs of a colony were normally administered by the *duoviri,* annual magistrates who often took great pride in calling themselves *praetores* or *strategoi.* The praetores of Philippi seemed to have judged the affair as an act of treason, and it is a legitimate question to ask why the Apostle did not claim his rights and privileges as a Roman citizen, especially since he did so on other occasions. Perhaps he did and his statement "civis Romanus sum" was either not heard or purposely ignored. At any rate, since the narrative in the first person plural suddenly ends, we must assume that St. Luke was not arrested and did not accompany the Apostle further. What happened to St. Paul? Glimpses of his experiences are recorded in his letters, where he speaks of how he and Silas "had already suffered and been shamefully treated at Philippi" (I Thess. 2:2), and he reminded his Corinthian congregation how he had "been beaten with rods" (II Cor. 11:25).

The following account, which speaks of nocturnal prayers, a sudden earthquake unfastening the prisoners chains, the care which the prisoners took for the jailer and the prevention of his attempted suicide and, finally, the conversion and baptism not only of the jailer but also of his entire household, contains a wealth of early Christian motifs which we later find repeatedly in the lives of the saints and martyrs of the persecuted Church.

> But about midnight Paul and Silas were praying and singing hymns to God, and the prisoners were listening to them, and suddenly there was a great earthquake, so that the foundations of the prison were shaken; and immediately all the doors were opened and every one's fetters were unfastened. When the jailer woke and saw that the prison doors were open, he drew his sword and was about to kill himself, supposing that the prisoners had escaped. But Paul cried with

a loud voice, "Do not harm yourself, for we are all here." And he called for lights and rushed in, and trembling with fear he fell down before Paul and Silas, and brought them out and said, "Men, what must I do to be saved?" And they said, "Believe in the Lord Jesus, and you will be saved, you and your household." And they spoke the word of the Lord to him and to all that were in his house. And he took them the same hour of the night, and washed their wounds, and he was baptized at once, with all his family. Then he brought them up into his house, and set food before them; and he rejoiced with all his household that he had believed in God.

Acts 16:25-34

Whatever the prisoners may have shared in the inner prison, it is most probable that they joined in the singing of the Psalms of David, which speak so eloquently of the sufferings of the imprisoned:

Hear my prayer, O Lord; and let my cry come to thee! Do not hide thy face from me in the day of my distress!... From heaven the Lord looked at the earth, to hear the groans of the prisoners, to set free those who were doomed to die.

Psalm 102:2, 19, 20

Let the groans of the prisoners come before thee; according to thy great power preserve those doomed to die.

Psalm 79:11

We are not told who the other prisoners were listening to the Apostle, but obviously the Apostle had transformed the dungeon into a chapel. As if in response to their prayer, there was a great earthquake which shook the foundations of the prison, breaking the gates and loosing everyone's chains. The effect upon the jailer was extreme, for he tried to follow the example of Cassius, Titinius his messenger, and Brutus, all of whom committed suicide in Philippi. The jailer, however, was deterred from his intent, and he was saved in more than one way. He and his household accepted the Lord Jesus and were baptized without delay. As did Lydia of Thyatira, the jailer also invited the missionaries into his home where, like the Good Samaritan on the Jerusalem-Jericho road, he washed their wounds and fed them. Nature and the soul of the jailer trembled on this eventful night. Just as the earthquake set the captives free, so the confrontation with the power of God in Jesus Christ gave a new vision to the jailer, a life of true freedom in Christ.

A local tradition identifies a Roman cistern as the place where St. Paul was imprisoned. This cistern is immediately east of what is known as Basilica A, north of the modern road which cuts through the ruins of Philippi. This "jail" is divided into two rooms, the outer and the inner prison (Acts 16:24). The guard will even point out where the chains which tied the prisoners were fastened to the wall.

> But when it was day, the magistrates sent the police, saying, "Let those men go." And the jailer reported the words to Paul, saying, "The magistrates have sent to let you go; now therefore come out and go in peace." But Paul said to them, "They have beaten us publicly, uncondemned, men who are Roman citizens, and have thrown us into prison; and do they now cast us out secretly? No! let them come themselves and take us out." The police reported these words to the magistrates, and they were afraid when they heard that they were Roman citizens; so they came and apologized to them. And they took them out and asked them to leave the city. So they went out of the prison, and visited Lydia; and when they had seen the brethren, they exhorted them and departed.
>
> Acts 16:35-40

Philippi: Basilica B

Much more must have happened during that memorable night than we shall ever know. One day the missionaries were taken into custody; the following day they were released. Was it, perhaps, the earthquake which had roused superstitious fears? Had the magistrates realized that they had flogged a Roman citizen without due investigation? In this they had broken two of the laws they were commissioned to uphold. First, they had condemned the missionaries without trial and, second, they had exposed the missionaries to public insult before the non-Roman population of the colony. Insult had been added to injustice, and St. Paul demanded an apology. Publicly they were declared guilty, publicly he expected to be pronounced innocent. The rights and privileges of a Roman citizen were important, especially in a Roman colony, but the Apostle also must have considered his witness to Jesus Christ. That he and Silas behaved like law-abiding citizens and did not attempt to escape from the prison at night must have left a lasting impression upon the small Christian community of Philippi. Wishing to avoid any further trouble, St. Paul and Silas followed the advice of the magistrates and left the city. St. Luke and Timothy, apparently, stayed behind in Philippi. Timothy rejoined St. Paul and Silas, if not in Thessalonica, then at least in Veria, before the Apostle left for Athens (Acts 17:14). St. Luke rejoined the Apostle on his return to Philippi.

ST. PAUL WRITES TO THE PHILIPPIANS

During his second visit to Ephesus, from the fall of 54 until the summer of 57, the Apostle suffered many trials and tribulations leading finally to his imprisonment in the city of Diana-Artemis. Epaphroditus, a member of the church in Philippi, visit-

Philippi: Entrance to the traditional prison

ed him there and brought him gifts from his friends in Macedonia (Phil. 4:18). Several years had passed since St. Paul's first visit to Philippi, but over the years he had kept in touch with his newly-founded congregations in Greece, and the most loyal of them was the fellowship which met beside the river. The Philippians must have heard about St. Paul's predicament. They had been partners in the building of Christ's kingdom in a very special way.

> And you Philippians yourselves know that in the beginning of the gospel, when I left Macedonia, no church entered into partnership with me in giving and receiving except you only.
>
> Phil. 4:15

Even when he was in Thessalonica, his next stopping place after having left Philippi, the Philippians had sent money on more than one occasion (Phil. 4:16), and after he had left Macedonia and went on to Athens and finally to Corinth, no church but theirs had helped him. While in Corinth, St. Paul graciously accepted the aid bestowed upon him by the Philippians (II Cor. 11:9), which seems to have made the Corinthians jealous of their Macedonian brethren.

When the Philippians, who were eternally grateful to the Apostle, heard of his imprisonment in Ephesus, they raised a fund and sent one of their number, Epaphroditus, to wait on him. It is true that the Acts of the Apostles does not mention an Ephesian imprisonment, and all that we know from his own writings is that he was kept in custody by the praetorian guard (Phil. 1:13). In I Corinthians St. Paul mentions having fought with beasts in Ephesus (15:32) and the apocryphal Acts of Paul informs us that at night he escaped unnoticed from his Ephesian prison to baptize two of his disciples, Eubola and Artemilla, in the nearby sea. From the middle of the 17th century onwards Western travelers more or less unanimously mention the "Prison of St. Paul" in Ephesus, a watchtower which was part of the city-wall built by Lysimachus in 286 B.C.

To appreciate the Apostle's ministry in Philippi one ought to read his letters to his converts in the Macedonian city. We use the plural "letters," advisedly, although the New Testament lists only one Letter to the Philippians. We believe that this one letter is, in fact, a combination of two letters. This idea finds some corroboration in the fact that Polycarp of Smyrna, writing to the Philippians only some eighty years later, speaks about "letters" written by St. Paul to them (3:2). St. Paul's first letter to the church in Philippi (Phil. 3:2-4:23) refers to the arrival of Epaphroditus with the thoughtful gifts of the Philippians. It is a thank-you-letter which, however, begins with a vigorous denunciation of the Judaizers, contrasting their legalistic attitude with his reliance upon Christ. It is in his conclusion that the Apostle acknowledged what the Philippians had done for him.

While in Ephesus, Epaphroditus, who had become very useful to the Apostle, fell ill (Phil. 2:25-30). News of his illness reached Philippi, and the Philippian Christians were much distressed. Epaphroditus recovered at least enough to return to his native city, carrying another letter to his congregation (Phil. 1:1-3:1). This letter begins with an expression of St. Paul's deep attachment to the members of the congregation in Philippi, who had been his most loyal friends. He hoped to send Timothy to them to receive a first-hand account of the situation in Philippi but, for the time being, he sent Epaphroditus, who had been to him like a brother as well as the messenger whom they had sent to see to his wants (Phil. 2:19).

The story of these two letters, which may have been written several months apart, is a wonderful testimony to the Apostle's relationship with his church in Philippi. Epaphroditus came with considerable gifts for the Apostle and returned, probably months later, with one of the most beautiful and meaningful passages written by the Apostle.

ST. PAUL'S SECOND VISIT

> Paul...took leave of them and departed for Macedonia.
>
> Acts 20:1

Perhaps in the same year the Apostle fulfilled his intentions as expressed in Acts 19:21 to revisit his congregations in Macedonia. We do not know which route he took from Ephesus but, probably, he went via Troy where he had not preached on his first visit but where he found a door opened to him as stated in II Cor. 2:12. Apparently he waited in Troy for Titus, who had been sent on a mission to Corinth, but since he did not come St. Paul left the city for Macedonia, probably sailing again to Neapolis and then on to Philippi. Here, finally, Titus joined the Apostle, bringing good news from Corinth (II Cor. 7:6-16) to which St. Paul responded with the letter to the Corinthians preserved in I Cor. 1-7. St. Paul soon wrote again to the Corinthians, especially in view of their response to his appeal for a collection for the church in Jerusalem. This letter constitutes chapters eight and nine of II Corinthians, and was delivered to the church in Corinth by Titus "who is famous among all the churches for his preaching of the gospel" (II Cor. 8:18).

After leaving Philippi the Apostle probably visited the churches in Thessalonica and Veria. If in fact he paid the visit to Illyricum which some people interpret from Romans 15:19, it may have been at this time that he did so. Eventually he continued south, but again we are not informed of any details although it is certain that he visited Corinth where he stayed for three months.

ST. PAUL'S THIRD VISIT

> And when a plot was made against him by the Jews as he was about to set sail for Syria, he determined to return through Macedonia. Sopater of Beroea, the son of Pyrrhus, accompanied him; and of the Thessalonians, Aristarchus and Secundus.
>
> Acts 20:3-4

We know nothing of the plot which deterred St. Paul from sailing from Corinth to Syria. Although made under duress, however, the Apostle's decision to visit the churches in Macedonia for a third time enabled him to collect the various delegates who were to accompany him to Jerusalem. Undoubtedly, these representatives were sent by the Macedonian churches to the Mother Church in Jerusalem to deliver the collection, of which the Apostle had admonished them again and again. As B.H.Streeter so clearly states:

> The Gentile churches were to be made to feel the essential unity of the Church by realizing their debt to, and their unity with the Mother Church; the Mother Church was to recognize the Gentile communities as true daughters of Israel.

The ruins of Philippi can be easily reached from Kavalla on the ancient Via Egnatia, which connected the East with Rome. From the port of Neapolis the route led west through Macedonia and Illyria to Dyrrachium on the Adriatic Sea. From Dyrrachium travelers sailed to Brundisium in Italy and then traveled overland to Rome. The old Roman road ran directly through Philippi on almost the same line as the modern highway. A section of it, where it intersected the city wall at the northwestern edge of Philippi, has been laid bare. The traveler who wants to retrace the steps of the Apostle should visit the market place where the missionaries were dragged before the magistrates. Known in Greek as the agora and in Latin as the forum, this place lay between the basilica and the acropolis. It has been completely uncovered and one can easily see the regular outlines. On the northern side is a rectangular podium to which steps gave access on two sides. It is probably this tribunal from which orators and politicians delivered their speeches, and where the magistrates convened to dispense justice. Although, as stated above, the ruins of the forum date back only to the 2nd century A.D., there is, nevertheless, good reason to assume that the plan of the agora changed very little from the days of the Apostle.

Thessalonica

> Now when they had passed through Amphipolis and Apollonia, they came to Thessalonica, where there was a synagogue of the Jews.
>
> Acts 17:1

ARRIVAL

Amphipolis was the capital of Macedonia Prima, the region east of the Strymon River, to which Philippi also belonged. It is about thirty miles west southwest of Philippi and, therefore, further than a normal day's journey, unless St. Paul and Silas did part of the journey on horseback. The lion of Amphipolis, which was erected apparently in the first half of the 4th century B.C. to commemorate some as yet unidentified victory, must have been a striking landmark also in the days of St. Paul. Excavations in Amphipolis in 1920 exposed the foundations of several early Christian basilicas. Today, Amphipolis is on the road from Thessalonica to Kavalla, sixty-six miles from Thessalonica. The ancient town stood on a hill and commanded the defile leading from the sea to the Strymon plain.

The missionaries proceeded to Thessalonica, the capital of the region of Macedonia Secunda. The city was founded by Cassander, who named it after his wife Thessalonike, the sister of Alexander the Great. Cicero was in exile here in 58 B.C., and Antony and Octavius were here after their victory at Philippi. In the first century A.D. Thessalonica was the most populous town of Macedonia and, before the founding of Constantinople, it was practically the capital of Greece, Illyricum, and Macedonia. In gratitude for the cooperation the inhabitants offered Antony and Octavius in their struggle against Cassius and Brutus, Thessalonica was made a free city like Athens. This meant that there were no Roman soldiers stationed in it and the government was in the hands of an assembly of the people, from whom the magistrates, known here as the politarchs, were chosen.

Whereas there was neither a synagogue in Amphipolis nor in Apollonia, we are told that here in Thessalonica St. Paul went to the synagogue where he preached for three Sabbaths. We do not know the size of the Jewish community at that time. The fact that until very recently Thessalonica had a large Jewish community is no reason to assume that a large Jewish community existed there in the first century A.D. The expulsion of the Jews from Spain during the reigns of Ferdinand V (1479-1516) and Isabella (1474-1504), caused many Jews to settle in the Ottoman Empire. From the early 16th century there were many Jews living in Thessalonica, and by 1699 when Paul Lucas, Louis XIV's emissary, visited the city there were thirty thousand of them, and twenty-two synagogues. Two hundred years later there were thirty-five thousand Jews and more than thirty-five synagogues in Thessalonica. Of the Jewish community at the time of St. Paul's visit, however, we know only that it existed and had a synagogue.

PREACHING

> And Paul went in, as was his custom, and for three weeks he argued with them from the scriptures, explaining and proving that it was necessary for the Christ to suffer and to rise from the dead, and saying, "This Jesus, whom I proclaim to you, is the Christ." And some of them were persuaded, and joined Paul and Silas; as did a great many of the devout Greeks and not a few of the leading women.

> Acts 17:2-4

St. Paul came to Thessalonica with Silas and, following his usual custom, he went to the synagogue where he used the Jewish scriptures as the source for his preaching. According to the Lukan account, the Apostle preached on the principal messianic issues, namely that the Old Testament prophets had spoken about a suf-

27

fering Messiah (Psalm 22; Isaiah 53); that after His death the Messiah would rise again; and that the crucified Jesus was, indeed, the Christ. In addition, however, we learn from St. Paul's own letters that he spoke about the glory of Christ's kingdom, for one of the accusations brought against the missionaries was that they had proclaimed "another king, Jesus" (Acts 17:7). From his subsequent correspondence with his newly founded church in Thessalonica it is evident that the message of the kingdom was central in his later preaching. St. Paul reminded the Thessalonians that his only purpose was to help them live lives "worthy of God, who calls you into his own kingdom and glory" (I Thess. 2:12). Moreover, the Apostle must have said a good deal about the Second Advent of Christ, for he referred explicitly to his preaching in Thessalonica when he asked them, "Do you not remember that when I was still with you I told you this?" (II Thess. 2:5).

Several years ago a bilingual stele was discovered near the Church of the Holy Virgin of Chalceon in the heart of Thessalonica. Its Greek text begins with

> The Lord said to Moses, "Say to Aaron and his sons,
> Thus you shall bless the people of Israel: you shall
> say to them,
> The Lord bless you and keep you;
> The Lord make his face to shine upon you
> and be gracious to you;
> The Lord lift up his countenance upon you,
> and give you peace.
>
> Numbers 6:22-26

The text goes on to mention the well-known sophist and rhetorician Sirikios, who was from Neapolis, a predominantly Samaritan city in Palestine. This leads us to believe that this stele may have belonged either to a proseuche or to a synagogue, perhaps

Thessalonica: The White Tower, built in the 15th century

even to a Samaritan synagogue. Although this particular stele belongs to the 4th or the beginning of the 5th century A.D., it is likely that the Jewish house of worship in question was built on the site of a former synagogue, which may have been the place where the Apostle "argued with them from the scriptures" for three Sabbaths.

The careful reader of St. Paul's letters to the Thessalonians and the Acts will notice a sharp difference of emphasis between the apostolic message delivered to the Jews in Thessalonica and that written later to the congregation. Should it be only a coincidence that St. Paul, who relied so heavily upon the Old Testament in his approach to the Jews of the city, should make no reference to the Jewish Scriptures in his two letters to the church in Thessalonica? This factor alone seems sufficient evidence that most of the new converts who gathered in the church in Thessalonica were not Jews, but Gentiles.

St. Paul devoted three weeks to reasoning with the Jews, winning some converts. These three weeks should be understood as the period at the beginning of his stay, during which he devoted himself exclusively to work among the Jews. When he turned to the Gentiles, however, he began to win large numbers of converts for Christ. He addressed "a great many" Greeks and, almost as a climax, "not a few of the leading women." We believe that this indicates a fairly long stay among the Gentiles of Thessalonica. The familiarity of his later correspondence with the congregation is such as could only have been gained by a prolonged stay, and the fact that he settled down at his trade as a tent-maker while in the city (Phil. 4:16) further indicates a longer stay, perhaps even of months, than the two or three weeks mentioned in Acts 17:2.

OPPOSITION

> But the Jews were jealous, and taking some wicked fellows of the rabble, they gathered a crowd, set the city in an uproar, and attacked the house of Jason, seeking to bring them out to the people. And when they could not find them, they dragged Jason and some of the brethren before the city

authorities, crying, "These men who have turned the world upside down have come here also, and Jason has received them; and they are all acting against the decrees of Caesar, saying that there is another king, Jesus." And the people and the city authorities were disturbed when they heard this. And when they had taken security from Jason and the rest, they let them go.

Acts 17:5-9

The Apostle's success among the Gentiles of Thessalonica had roused the enmity of the Jews, who may have felt that their influence in the city was being threatened or undermined. As in Iconium and Lystra (Acts 14), they employed the worthless idlers who can be found in every city and assaulted the house of Jason. Jason was probably a Hellenistic Jew, whose real name may well have been Joshua. St. Paul and Silas were absent, however, so the crowd dragged Jason and some other Christians before the magistrates. As in the case of Philippi, so also in this case we should keep in mind that the missionaries, because of the recent expulsion of the Jews from Rome, were particularly susceptible to the charge of treason. The seriousness of the events in Thessalonica is reflected in the Apostle's own writings, in which he speaks of much affliction (I Thess. 1:6), and of the Gospel having been advanced against great opposition (I Thess. 2:2). At any rate, the result was that the missionaries left the city for Veria.

There is no agreement concerning the traditional place of the Apostle's preaching in Thessalonica. When the English traveler Richard Pococke passed through the city during the first part of the 18th century, he was told that St. Paul had preached on the site occupied by the subterranean church within the Church of St. Demetrius, which in his days was "the most beautiful mosque in the town." Conybeare, about one hundred years later, wrote that a local tradition maintained that the Church of St. Demetrius was built on the ruins of the ancient synagogue where the Apostle reasoned with the Jews. Some Thessalonians assign the site of St. Paul's preaching to a place near the 5th century Rotunda of St. George, especially in view of the fact that the street which passes this church is named after the Apostle. In the 8th century Church of Haghia Sophia a stone rostrum used to be pointed out as the spot from which St. Paul was believed to have delivered his sermons. More recently guides pointed out St. Paul's pulpit, half of which stood in the courtyard of the Church of St. George, while the other half stood outside the Church of St. Panteleimon.

Finally, there is the tradition reported by H.V. Morton that when the Apostle came from Philippi to Thessalonica he visited a house in the upper town, undoubtedly that of Jason, which since the early Middle Ages had been occupied by the Monastery of Vlattadon. However, none of these traditions are seriously upheld by biblical scholars.

There are two churches of St. Paul in Thessalonica which preserve the memory of the Apostle's ministry, and both are in the suburb which bears his name. Late in the 19th century the Greeks established a charitable association in this suburb and later built a chapel in honor of the Apostle to serve it. This chapel, however, did not serve the steadily increasing community. One night in the 1950's, the story goes, the mayor of the suburb had a dream in which St. Paul appeared and told him to build another church, so a new Church of St. Paul was built nearby, behind the municipal hospital. On the grounds of the old chapel are the spring and the so-called cave which sheltered the Apostle, surrounded by several tall cedars. Some people believe that the chapel stands on the site of the old synagogue, but others maintain that here, outside the walls of the ancient city, the Apostle spent the night when he was driven from Thessalonica.

ST. PAUL WRITES TO THE THESSALONIANS

Only a few weeks passed before the church in Thessalonica received its first letter from the Apostle. This letter was written by St. Paul in Corinth, where he had resumed his preaching, so we may assign it to the late spring or summer of the year 50. He was still thinking about the congregations in Thessalonica and Philippi, wondering about the developments among the brethren whom he was compelled to leave behind. His principal interest, of course, was in the continuation of the church.

Timothy, whom the Apostle had left in Philippi, had joined St. Paul in Veria and had traveled with him to Athens. Instead of keeping Timothy with him, however, St. Paul's anxiety about the Macedonian churches compelled him to send Timothy back to Thessalonica. Timothy left St. Paul in Athens and returned north to strengthen the new churches in their troubles (I Thess. 3:1-2).

The purpose of this First Letter to the Thessalonians was to reply to the good news which Timothy had brought with him on his return to St. Paul in Corinth (I Thess. 3:6). The Apostle was understandably encouraged and, in gratitude to these good tidings, he dictated a letter to one of the numerous letter-writers available in every city in Greece. (That St. Paul did not write his letters with his own hand is evident from the references in Rom. 16:22, where the amanuensis Tertius is mentioned, and in II Thess. 3:17.) The situation, however, which Timothy had observed in Thessalonica was not altogether good. Charges had been brought against St. Paul, and the Apostle defended himself against the unjust accusations. Timothy reported other difficulties among the Thessalonians in addition to these charges. He told of the ill-treatment the converts had received from their old friends, so the Apostle reminded them of their fellowship in suffering with the churches in Judaea (I Thess. 2:14). In his relationship with the Thessalonians, St. Paul appears as the true shepherd who is deeply concerned about the spiritual and moral life of his sheep. This concern is reflected in his admonitions about their sexual conduct, their married life (I Thess. 4:3-8). As did the Apostle, the Thessalonians expected the early return of Christ, and in response to these expectations and questions St. Paul reassured them that really no one knows when the Lord will return, for he "will come like a thief in the night" (I Thess. 5:2).

The recipients of this letter could not have realized that they held the first piece of New Testament literature in their hands. St. Paul's First Letter to the Thessalonians, written less than twenty years after Christ's resurrection, is the oldest New Testament document. It throws considerable light upon the relations between the Apostle and his new converts. They are friends, but of a special kind; they are friends in Christ.

Several weeks if not even some months had passed after St. Paul wrote his First Letter to the Thessalonians when, while the Apostle was preaching to his newly established community in Corinth, news reached him that some of the Thessalonian brethren looked so intensely forward to the return of Christ that they had ceased work and were pursuing a life of religious contemplation. These drones were becoming a scandal in the community because they refused to work and obliged the other Christians to support them. That this tendency had existed before is evident from St. Paul's warning in his First Letter to the Thessalonians. In this second letter the Apostle went to great length to convince his readers that the time had not yet come, since the "man of lawlessness" or the Antichrist had not yet appeared. He admonished the idlers to return to work and earn their living. Repeating the command which he had given them while he was among them, he very bluntly said: "If any one will not work, let him not eat" (II Thess. 3:10). The last word of greeting the Apostle added with his own hand.

The fact that we may find these letters difficult to understand merely underlines their situational character. Therefore, we can do no better than attempt to reconstruct the situation so as to reap the maximum benefit of the wisdom contained in these writings.

Veria

The brethren immediately sent Paul and Silas away by night to Beroea; and when they arrived they went into the Jewish synagogue. Now these Jews were more noble than those in Thessalonica, for they received the word with all eagerness, examining the scriptures daily to see if these things were so. Many of them therefore believed, with not a few Greek women of high standing as well as men. But when the Jews of Thessalonica learned that the word of God was proclaimed by Paul at Beroea also, they came there too, stirring up and inciting the crowds. Then the brethren immediately sent Paul off on his way to the sea, but Silas and Timothy remained there.

Acts 17:10-14

We have no details of the nocturnal escape route taken by the Apostle and Silas from Thessalonica. Probably they passed through the Arch of Augustus and the Western Gate and then continued along the Via Egnatia. If they took the road that ran almost directly westward they would have reached Veria, which is about fifty miles from Thessalonica, in approximately three days. This city, situated on the eastern slope of Mount Vermion, commands an extensive view of the plain which is irrigated by the waters of the Haliacmon and Axius rivers. In 168 B.C. when the Romans defeated Macedonia, they made Veria the capital of one of the four republics into which they divided the kingdom. In addition to the Macedonian population, a fair number of Romans and Jews must have lived in the city.

When St. Paul arrived in Veria he went, according to his custom, immediately to the synagogue where, to his pleasant surprise, he discovered that these Jews were "more noble" than those he had encountered in Thessalonica. Their minds were open and they were willing to receive the truth provided, however, that the Holy Scriptures substantiated the assertions made by the Apostle. They examined the Scriptures themselves to see if St. Paul's arguments were justified by the Old Testament prophecies. Just as in the case of the Apostle's ministry in Thessalonica, so also in Veria many non-Jews were attracted to his preaching. In addition to the Jews who accepted the new faith, there were "not a few" high born Greek women and men who also became Christians.

We do not know how long the Apostle stayed in Veria. The reference to the daily searching of the Holy Scriptures by the Jews indicates that he remained there at least for several days.

In I Thess. 2:18, St. Paul spoke of his desire to return to his brethren in Thessalonica, and he might, then, have lingered as long as possible in the neighborhood of Thessalonica. On the other hand, however, the Jews of Thessalonica probably did not delay coming to Veria as soon as they heard of the Apostle's success there among their fellow believers. Therefore, after not too long a time, St. Paul was forced to leave Veria, but he left Silas and Timothy behind to strengthen the faith of the new converts and to organize the church.

Some of the new converts apparently accompanied the Apostle on his way to the coast, where he took a ship to Athens. It was probably Dium, at that time the Roman colony known as Colonia Julia Diensis, near the base of Mt. Olympus, from which the Apostle sailed. As W.J. Conybeare points out: "No city is more likely than Dium to have been the last, as Philippi was the first, through which St. Paul passed on his journey through the provinces."

On the other hand, there is an interesting addition made by the 5th century Bezan or Western text of the Acts of the Apostles according to which the Apostle traveled by road to Athens, although "he neglected Thessaly, for he was prevented from preaching the word unto them" (Acts 17:15). When William M. Leake, the famous 19th century British antiquarian and topographer, passed the town of Servia near Veria, the bishop assured him "that St. Paul had passed through Servia on his way from Veria to Athens." Today, however, neither the local clergy nor the inhabitants remember this tradition.

The memory of the Apostle's ministry to the people of Veria is kept alive by an impressive monument built in his honor. In the southeastern section of the city, not far from the road leading to Kozane, there is a beautiful white marble monument enshrining a mosaic representing the Apostle Paul. Here, according to

Veria: Monument (*kouvouklion*) commemorating St. Paul's preaching in the city

the local tradition, were the steps from which the Apostle delivered his sermons.

According to some people in Veria, Sopater, the son of Pyrrhus, was the first convert in the church in Veria. His name is mentioned by St. Luke in connection with St. Paul's third missionary journey (Acts 20:4). On the other hand, the Greek Orthodox Calendar of Saints, the Synaxar, refers to Karpus, one of the Seventy Disciples, as being the first bishop of this city.

A visit to Veria should include some of the thirty-seven late Byzantine churches which are found all over the city. Many of these churches contain fine frescos.

ACHAIA

Athens

> Those who conducted Paul brought him as far as Athens; and receiving a command for Silas and Timothy to come to him as soon as possible, they departed. Now while Paul was waiting for them at Athens, his spirit was provoked within him as he saw that the city was full of idols.
>
> Acts 17:15-16

Passing the island of Euboea, the ship carrying the Apostle soon reached the southern extremity of Attica, known as Cape Colonna because of the white columns of the Temple of Poseidon, which still are a landmark for all passing sailors. After sailing around Cape Sounion, St. Paul would have seen to port first the island of Aegina and then that of Salamis, while to starboard his eyes must have fallen on Hymettus, the mountain range rising close to the shore. Coming closer to Piraeus, he would have seen Lycabettus and the Acropolis, and he would have joined the sailors who eagerly looked out·for the gilded point of the spear which the statue of Athena Promachos held high on top of the Acropolis. For every traveler this statue, whose helmet rose approximately thirty feet above her sandals, was the first sight of Athens.

A recent local tradition places the Apostle's landing in Glyphada, near the Antonopoulos restaurant, where there are ruins of an early Christian basilica. Another local tradition has him land in Phaleron. The site of the temple of the unknown god, which he passed on his way to Athens, is believed by some people to be marked by the chapel of the Sts. Theodoroi, which is near the Panionios soccer field in Nea Smyrni. It is much more likely, however, that his ship docked at Piraeus which, even in the days of the Apostle, was one of the busiest harbors in Greece, and that he proceeded to the city along the same route later followed by Pausanias (2nd century A.D.).

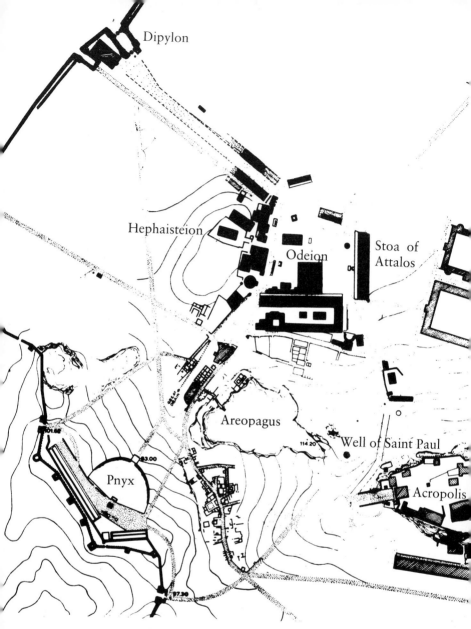

Athens: Plan of the Agora at the time of St. Paul

Source: The American School of Classical Studies in Athens

In the *Life of Apollonius of Tyana* by Philostratus, there is a passage which fits the arrival of St. Paul in Athens beautifully:

> Having come to anchor in the Piraeus, he went up from the harbor to the city. Advancing onward, he met several of the philosophers. In his first conversation, finding the Athenians much devoted to Religion, he discoursed on sacred subjects. This was at Athens, where also altars of Unknown Gods are set up.

W.J. Conybeare speaks of this extract from the biography of Apollonius as being a "suitable and comprehensive motto to that passage in St. Paul's biography on which we are now entering." If a summary of the 17th chapter of the Acts of the Apostles had been required, it could not have been better expressed. The city visited by Apollonius was the very Athens visited by the Apostle.

Piraeus under the Romans still showed the remains of the fortifications which Themistocles had built to fortify the harbor as an outpost of Athens. Over the centuries, however, these defenses had been neglected and had fallen into decay. The Long Walls which connected Piraeus with Athens in the classical age had also fallen into ruin. If St. Paul took the same route as Pausanias, the traveler of about a century later, he would have gone north from the harbor of Piraeus and have entered Athens by the "Dipylon" or the "Double Gate" on the west side of the city, where the roads from Piraeus, Corinth, the Academy, and Boeotia converged. Before passing the gate, however, he would have gone through an extensive cemetery, where he would have noticed the graves of many distinguished Athenian citizens, the most famous being Menander, the son of Diopithes, for it was the custom to bury the dead outside the city walls alongside the principal roads. This district was also referred to as the "outer keramikos," because of the potters' quarter which had been located here. With Pausanias as our guide, we can easily describe the objects seen by the Apostle. Passing through the Dipylon, St. Paul would have seen the Temple of Demeter with statues of the goddess, her daughter, and Iacchus, all of which were the work of Praxiteles, and a little further on he would have passed the statue of an equestrian Poseidon hurling his trident. Beyond this, he would have seen the statues of Healing Athena, Zeus, Apollo, and Hermes standing near the Sanctuary of Dionysus.

To the best of our knowledge St. Paul paid only one visit to Athens, but it was an important event as described by St. Luke. The ancient glory of this city had already vanished. In sharp contrast to modern Athens with its busy streets, Athens two thousand years ago was merely a provincial university city, the home of art treasures. In general, Rome respected the city for its illustrious past. Most of Greece had been plundered by the Roman governors, and even Athens had been sacked by Sulla in 86 B.C., but still the city of Pallas Athena could boast of the magnificent monuments so eloquently described by Pausanias. While the Apostle waited for Silas and Timothy, whom he had instructed to join him as soon as possible, he must have explored the city in the same manner in which tourists do today, although with one difference we must not overlook. Today's tourists are generally sympathetic to Homeric religion and appreciate the splendor of classical Greece considerably more than a Cilician Jew like St. Paul, to whom, for example, the strife between Athena and Poseidon for the possession of the city must have appeared the height of blasphemy. The Apostle would certainly not have shared the view of the later Christian fathers, who saw in Athens "the rudiments of Paradise."

The Apostle would have visited the Royal Colonnade, the Metroum or Sanctuary of the Mother of the Gods with her image, the work of Phidias, and the nearby Council House of the Five Hundred with its numerous statues. In the agora the Apostle would have passed what Pausanias called "the Music Hall at Athens," the odeum, a small roofed theater. In the agora the Athenians had an altar of Mercy, which stood in a grove of laurels and olives. "Humanity is not the only characteristic of

Athens: The Church of the Holy Apostles

the Athenians," says Pausanias, "they are also more pious than other people, for they have altars of Modesty, of Rumour, and of Impulse." Close to the agora, in the gymnasium of Ptolemy, there was a stone statue of Hermes, and a bronze statue of Ptolemy. Wherever the Apostle turned, he must have seen statues, temples, and shrines. There was the Sanctuary of the Dioscuri, the Serapeum in the lower part of the city, the Temple of Olympian Zeus southeast of the Acropolis, the Pythium on the southern side of the Acropolis, the Sanctuary of Dionysus at the very foot of the Acropolis, and many more.

We can assume that St. Paul visited the Acropolis at least once. Entering through the Propylaea, which is still one of the most splendid monuments of ancient Greece, he would have passed two statues of horsemen facing each other on opposite sides of the road. On his right, on the western edge of the Acropolis, was the Temple of Victory Athena, the so-called Wingless Victory. As had Pausanias and all other visitors to the Acropolis, St. Paul would have looked towards the sea and seen the Bay of Phaleron, perhaps with grain ships from Alexandria or the Euxine. He would have visited the most famous and beautiful of all Greek temples, the Parthenon, and then the Erechtheum standing on the northern edge of the Acropolis. Here his eyes must have fallen on the oldest and most venerated statue of Athena, which like that of Diana of Ephesus, was believed to have fallen from heaven (Acts 19:35). Finally, there was the most conspicuous statue of the city-goddess, a dedication from the spoils of the Battle of Marathon. This image dominated all buildings of the Acropolis and could be seen easily even from Piraeus.

An ancient proverb declared that there were more gods in Athens than men, and wherever the Apostle looked, in niches and on pedestals, in temples and on street corners, were gods and demi-gods. Among this forest of deities the Apostle discovered one altar dedicated to the "unknown god." No well attested

Athens: The ancient Agora and Acropolis

examples of a similar dedication in the singular form are known to us in literary texts or in inscriptions, although there are several instances in the plural form. Pausanias wrote that on the road from Phaleron to Athens he saw "altars of gods called unknown." Oecumenius, the Greek commentator on the Acts of the Apostles, stated that the full inscription on the Athenian altar was: "To the gods of Asia and Europe and Libya, to the Unknown and Strange Gods," while Tertullian in his commentary retains the plural form, "to Unknown Gods." The idea, of course, was that these altars to the "unknown gods" ensured that no deity was omitted from worship. We have something similar in our Christian tradition. On November 1st many Christian churches celebrate the Feast of All Saints, thereby commemorating all those martyrs and confessors whose names are not especially mentioned throughout the liturgical year.

At any rate, the Apostle must have been appalled as he looked upon all this idolatry for, after all, he had been reared in the tradition which postulated "You shall have no other gods before me; You shall not make for yourself a graven image, or any likeness of anything that is in heaven above, or that is in the earth beneath, or that is in the water under the earth; you shall not bow down to them or serve them" (Ex. 20:3, 4). He turned to his task and preached first in the synagogue, then in the agora, and finally he spoke before the Council of the Areopagus.

PREACHING

So he argued in the synagogue with the Jews and the devout persons, and in the market place every day with those who chanced to be there. Some also of the Epicurean and Stoic philosophers met him. And some said, "What would this babbler say?" Others said,"He seems to be a preacher of foreign divinities" — because he preached Jesus and the resurrection. And they took hold of him and brought him to the Areopagus, saying, "May we know what this new

Lamp with menorah, found in the Athens agora

Courtesy of the Agora Excavations of the American School of Classical Studies at Athens

Marie Mauzy

teaching is which you present? For you bring some strange things to our ears; we wish to know therefore what these things mean." Now all the Athenians and the foreigners who lived there spent their time in nothing except telling or hearing something new.

Acts 17:17-21

No archaeological evidence has yet been discovered that would help us locate the synagogue in which the Apostle argued.

The earliest Jewish find discovered in Athens is a mid-fourth-century A.D. lamp with a relief of what may be a seven-branched candlestick (menorah). A Pentellic marble stele also found in Athens depicts a menorah flanked by a shofar on the left and a lulav on the right.

Although Athens was no longer the one predominant center of philosophical thought as it had been during the Classical period,

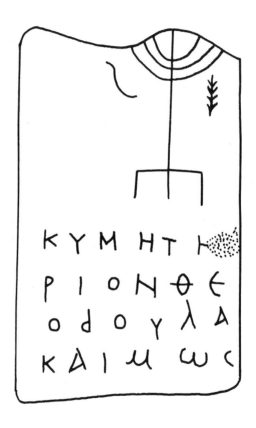

Drawing of figures on marble stele depicting shofar on left and lulav on right of menorah

philosophy as such still maintained her seat in the city of Socrates. The great schools, the Academy, the Lyceum, the Garden, and the Porch still operated as in previous years. The agora still served as a meeting place for the Athenian population. Here Demosthenes had rebuked the Athenians for their customary idle talk, exhorting them that they were always discussing news and excitement when their very constitution was being threatened. Here, still, in the days of St. Paul, they "spent their time in nothing except telling or hearing something new." The Stoic philosophers had their school, the Stoa Poecile or the Painted Cloister, within the precincts of the agora, and the Epicureans had their school nearby. St. Paul was familiar with Stoic philosophy because in his native city had lived many Stoic philosophers, such as Antipater of Tarsus, Zeno of Tarsus, and Chrysippus, who was said to have been a native of Tarsus.

Most of St. Paul's listeners must have believed that the Apostle was upholding two new deities, Jesus and Anastasis, the resurrection, which to pagan listeners might well have sounded like the names of a god and a goddess. They called the Apostle a "spermologos," literally a "seed-picker," which in Athenian slang of the time was applied to those who loafed about the agora picking up odds and ends. It was probably the Epicurean faction which applied this description of contempt and derision to the Apostle. Other listeners were seriously concerned that he was introducing new objects of worship, and they wished to hear more. In addition, the more liberal and tolerant Stoics were eager to learn what this foreign teacher had to say, and so St. Paul was brought to the Areopagus.

According to Aeschylus, the Council of the Areopagus was founded by the goddess Athena herself. It had received its name from the "Hill of Ares," the god of war, on which its meetings were convened. Another explanation would make the Areopagus the hill of "Arai" (curses) because, according to this tradition, the first trial on the hill was that of Orestes, who had been cursed and hounded by the Furies for the murder of his mother.

In the days of the Apostle, the Council of the Areopagus had authority over all matters pertaining to the religious life of the city, and it was for this reason that St. Paul was summoned to

49

appear before this body. The Apostle was neither accused of any misconduct nor was he tried by the Council of the Areopagus. Hearing of the new doctrines advanced by St. Paul, the council felt obliged to gain first hand information. What they heard was one of the most famous speeches recorded in the New Testament.

AREOPAGUS

So Paul, standing in the middle of the Areopagus, said: "Men of Athens, I perceive that in every way you are very religious. For as I passed along, and observed the objects of your worship, I found also an altar with this inscription, 'To an unknown god.' What therefore you worship as unknown, this I proclaim to you. The God who made the world and everything in it, being Lord of heaven and earth, does not live in shrines made by man, nor is he served by human hands, as though he needed anything, since he himself gives to all men life and breath and everything. And he made from one every nation of men to live on all the face of the earth, having determined allotted periods and the boundaries of their habitation, that they should seek God, in the hope that they might feel after him and find him. Yet he is not far from each one of us, for

'In him we live and move and have our being:
as even some of your poets have said,
'For we are indeed his offspring.'
Being then God's offspring, we ought not to think that the Deity is like gold, or silver, or stone, a representation by the art and imagination of man. The times of ignorance God overlooked, but now he commands all men everywhere to repent, because he has fixed a day on which he will judge the world in righteousness by a man whom he has appointed, and of this he has given assurance to all men by raising him from the dead."

Acts 17:22-31

Lamp with image of St. Paul, found in the Athens agora

Marie Mauzy

This is not the place for a textual and critical analysis of the famous speech to the Areopagus. Modern New Testament scholarship has understood this speech as recorded by St. Luke as the product of the post-Pauline period. In it "the Lukan Paul" uses expressions and ideas which appear somewhat alien to un-contested Pauline literature, and we sympathize with the problem of reconciling its underlying philosophy with St. Paul's evangelical tenets as expressed during his stay in Corinth:

> When I came to you, brethren, I did not come proclaiming to you the testimony of God in lofty words or wisdom. For I decided to know nothing among you except Jesus Christ and him crucified . . . and my speech and my message were not in plausible words of wisdom, but in demonstration of

51

the Spirit and power, that your faith might not rest in the wisdom of men but in the power of God.

I Cor. 2:1-5

Nevertheless, the main approach of the Areopagus speech may well have been St. Paul's own in spite of the phrasing which may have been the free literary creation of the author of the Acts. For example, the quotation from the *Phenomena* by the poet Aratus "For we are indeed his offspring," could very well be Pauline. The works of this 3rd century B.C. poet no doubt were read in the schools of Tarsus where St. Paul studied in his youth. In speaking to the Jews of Pisidian Antioch, St. Paul traced God's purpose in their own history. Preaching to the pagans at Lystra, he spoke of God as revealed in nature. While speaking to the sophisticated Athenians he employed points of contact with his listeners' ways of thinking. As G.H.C. Macgregor points out, "the general tone and tenor of the speech are exactly what might be expected in the circumstances."

Recognizing that we may not possess the exact transcript of the Areopagus speech, it is noteworthy that the Early Church preserved apocryphal excerpts of the speech, which are not recorded by St. Luke. In his *Policraticus* John of Salisbury (1115-1180), the English diplomatist and bishop of Chartres, quotes several apocryphal passages of St. Paul's Areopagus speech.

> I find that the Apostle Paul when preaching to the Athenians strove to impress on their minds Jesus Christ and him crucified, that he might show by the example of heathens how the release of many came about through the shame of the cross ... No one could be found capable of freeing all, both Jews and Gentiles, save he unto whom the heathen are given for an inheritance, and such one could be no other than the Son of God. Then he proclaimed the shame of the cross in such a way as gradually to purge away the foolishness of the heathen ... The ingenuities of an Aristotle, the subtleties of a Chrysippus, the gins of all the philosophers were defeated by the rising of one who had been dead.

The place usually indicated for the meeting of the Council of the Areopagus is on the top of the hill, at the head of the flight of stairs leading up from the south. At the foot of the sixteen steps leading to the top of the rock is a copper plaque with the Greek text of the Areopagus speech. It is doubtful, however, that the Council would have convened on the very top of the hill, especially since the cuttings which remain suggest that houses or other small structures were there. Professor Eugene Vanderpool has suggested that the Council met on the site where, during the medieval period, stood the Church of St. Dionysius:

> Is it not reasonable to suppose that the early Christian community in Athens, in erecting on the Hill of Ares a church in honour of its first bishop and patron saint, St. Paul's first and most distinguished convert, would choose a site connected with the life of the saint, the Court of the Areopagus, by now abandoned, of which Dionysius had been a member and where he had been converted by the Apostle's stirring speech?
>
> Craig Mauzy

Athens: The Royal Stoa during recent excavations

However, excavations on the site of the Church of St. Dionysius have revealed no traces of the Council of the Areopagus. It is probable, therefore, that the council was located a little east of the church where there are now huge masses of rock fallen from the cliffs above, making excavations impossible.

Local tradition has identified some rock cuttings on the lower slopes of the Areopagus with the spot where St. Paul is said to have delivered his speech. One of the rooms, which shows a distinct cutting shaped in the form of a cross — actually made to receive an ancient statue or pillar — is especially singled out in this connection.

On the other hand, Demosthenes (325 B.C.) informs us that the Council of the Areopagus sometimes assembled in the Stoa Basilios (Royal Stoa), directly north of the Stoa of Zeus and according to Pausanias "the first on the right" in the agora. Some scholars maintain that the Apostle might have delivered his speech in the recently (1970) excavated Royal Stoa in the northwestern corner of the agora across the tracks of the Piraeus-

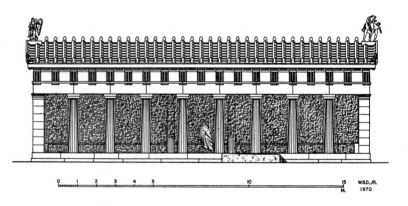

Restoration of the Royal Stoa
Source: *Hesperia* 40 (1971), p. 247

Kifissia railway line. The newly discovered stoa was one of the most venerable public buildings of ancient Athens. Situated at the intersection of the Panathenaic Way and the street bordering the western side of the square, this stoa was one of the smallest and simplest examples of Greek civic architecture. Its eastern façade had a colonnade of eight Doric columns, while the other three sides were enclosed by walls of solid masonry.

From the middle of the 17th century until the beginning of the 19th century a curious tradition circulated in Athens concerning the ‘Apostle's escape from the anger of the people following the conversion of Dionysius the Areopagite. From the days of Father Robert de Dreux, chaplain to the French ambassador (1669), down to Richard Chandler who visited Athens in 1765-66, Western travelers heard that the Apostle took refuge for a day or more in a well. The well, which was actually a

Ingrid Keller

Athens: The "Well of St. Paul" near the foundations of the apse of the Church of St. Dionysius

cistern, known in the 18th century as the "Arabian Well," was situated a few feet east of the apse of the former church of St. Dionysius the Areopagite at the foot of the Areopagus. Whether or not the Christians realized the improbability of a person hiding in a well, we do not know, but when J.C. Hobhouse and Lord Byron visited the Areopagus in 1810, they were shown instead one of the caves near the chapel of St. Dionysius where the Apostle was supposed to have found shelter.

RESULTS

> Now when they heard of the resurrection of the dead, some mocked; but others said, "We will hear you again about this." So Paul went out from among them. But some men joined him and believed, among them Dionysius the Areopagite and a woman named Damaris and others with them.
>
> Acts 17:32-34

Most commentators regard St. Paul's visit to Athens as a failure because he did not establish a Christian community in this city as he did elsewhere. Some of the listeners to his Areopagus speech obviously were contemptuous, some were interested, and others, like Dionysius the Areopagite and a woman named Damaris, were converted. About this woman named Damaris we know nothing. It is unlikely that she was a lady of noble birth, since such a distinction would probably have been recorded, as it had been in Thessalonica and Veria. It has been suggested that she was a foreigner, or perhaps she was a hetaera, a courtesan for the upper class. Dionysius is said to have become bishop of Athens, and is believed to have suffered martyrdom during the persecutions of the emperor Domitian in the last decade of the first century A.D. After the Apostle's departure from Athens, a curtain fell over Christianity in the city until a few generations later. We know only that a small Christian community did develop and grow in spite of the paganism which continued to flourish.

In 1889 James Rendel Harris, following in the steps of Konstantin von Tischendorf, went to the Monastery of St. Catherine in Sinai where he discovered a Syriac copy of the *Apology of Aristides*. Aristides, an Athenian philosopher of the beginning of the 2nd century, was an active and dedicated Christian in Athens. He is known for the famous *Apology* he addressed to the emperor Hadrian, in which he set forth in almost Pauline manner and style a rational and yet very simple appeal for the people to accept Jesus as their Christ. For that matter, Aristides' *Apology* reads in many ways like the Areopagus speech. Another 2nd century Athenian philosopher, Athenagoras, defended Christianity in an address to the emperors Marcus Aurelius and Commodus. The 4th century Greek sophist and rhetorician, Libanius, who taught St. John Chrysostomus and St. Basil of Caesarea, studied in the philosophical schools in Athens, as did St. Gregory the Theologian (ca. 329-388), one of the four great fathers of the Eastern Church. Athens remained an active center of Greek philosophical thought until 529 when the emperor Justinian ordered the city's philosophical schools to close.

During the reign of Theodosius II (408-450), whose wife Eudocia Augusta was an Athenian, several temples in Athens were converted into churches. The Sanctuary of Asklepios at the foot of the Acropolis, for example, became the Church of the Silverless Ones (Hagioi Anargyroi), Saints Cosmas and Damian, 3rd century physicians who refused payment for their services. During the reign of Justinian (527-565) the Parthenon was turned into a church and dedicated to the Holy Wisdom; later it was dedicated to the Holy Virgin. At about the same time the Erechtheion was converted into a church, and the greater part of the interior was destroyed in the alterations. In the 7th century a three aisled basilica was built on the site of an earlier church in the courtyard of the Library of Hadrian. An apse was added to the Hephaesteion and the building was dedicated to St. George. A *Te Deum* service was held in this Church of St. George on 13 December 1834 to celebrate King Otto's arrival in the new capital of independent Greece, and a centenary *Te Deum* was held here again exactly one hundred years later.

Other churches were constructed in and around the Temple of Olympian Zeus. West of the temple's propylaia are the remains of a three aisled 5th century basilica, which probably was dedicated to St. Nicholas. Another early church known as "St. John at the columns" was built within the columns on the east side of the temple. According to tradition a Christian ascetic lived in a tiny room built on the architrave over two columns of the temple. Many remains of Early Christian and Byzantine churches are exhibited in the inner court of the Byzantine Museum in Athens.

In the 12th century Anna Comnena wrote in her *Alexiad* of her father, Alexius I (1081-1118),

> that in the quarters near the Acropolis, where the mouth of the sea widens, he had discovered a very large church, dedicated to the great Apostle Paul, and here he built up a second city inside the queen of cities. For as this church was on the highest spot in the city it stood out like a citadel.

Although not situated "on the highest spot," it is likely that this is a reference to the Church of the Holy Apostles which stands below the Acropolis and opposite the Hephaesteion. Built between 1000 and 1025, this church was restored to something like its original state by the American School of Classical Studies in 1956.

Every June 29th, the Feast of Sts. Peter and Paul, a vesper service (hesperinos) is conducted upon the rock of the Areopagus. A large wooden cross is set up on the top of the rock behind a portable altar, which is flanked by an almost life-size icon of St. Paul. The Archbishop of Athens and All Greece, assisted by other bishops and priests, usually performs the ceremony.

Athens: Vesper service on the Areopagus

Although the Gospel was brought to Athens by St. Paul, it is not he but his first Athenian convert, St. Dionysius the Areopagite, who is venerated as the patron saint of Athens. The only Orthodox church in Athens bearing the name of the Apostle is on Psaron Street in the vicinity of the Larissa Railway Station. This church was dedicated on December 5, 1910 by the Metropolitan of Athens, H.B. Theocletos, and is adorned with wall paintings depicting the conversion of St. Paul and St. Paul in Athens. St. Paul is also commemorated in the modern Orthodox Church of St. Dionysius the Areopagite on Skoufa Street near Kolonaki Square. It has a beautiful mosaic and a wall painting of St. Paul on the Areopagus. The Anglican church on Philhellenon Street, built between 1838 and 1843 and designed by the Greek architect Stamatios Kleanthis, is dedicated to St. Paul. In the suburb of Kifissia, St. Paul's Catholic Church is at 4 Kokkinaki Street. In the German Evangelical Church at 66 Sina Street, one of the stained glass windows shows St. Paul in front of the Parthenon.

Corinth

> After this he left Athens and went to Corinth. And he found
> a Jew named Aquila, a native of Pontus, lately come from
> Italy with his wife Priscilla, because Claudius had com-
> manded all the Jews to leave Rome. And he went to see
> them; and because he was of the same trade he stayed with
> them, and they worked, for by trade they were tentmakers.

> Acts 18:1-3

There is no indication that St. Paul was driven out of Athens
either by the mob or by the authorities. He simply left the city
and went to Corinth, which was the capital of the Roman province of Greece, known as Achaia. Because Corinth had direct
communications with Rome and the West it was a strategic location for the spread of the Gospel. The number of Jews in
Corinth may have been another reason for the Apostle's selec-
tion of this city. Jews lived throughout the province of Achaia,
according to Philo "in most of the best parts of the Pelopon-
nese," but the largest Jewish community was in Corinth. Esti-
mates as high as 20,000 have been given for this community,
but since we have no literary evidence these figures are only
conjecture. Whatever their numbers, part of the reason for the
Jewish presence in Achaia may have been the difficulties the
Jews had experienced in Rome during the reign of the emperor
Claudius (41 B.C. - 54 A.D.).

We are not told how the Apostle traveled from Athens to
Corinth. The overland route, fairly closely following the route
of the modern highway from Athens to Corinth, ran along the
Sacred Way to Eleusis, through the Megarid, and along the steep
Scironian cliffs to the Isthmus of Corinth. It was a difficult
route, and yet it must have been well traveled. The journey

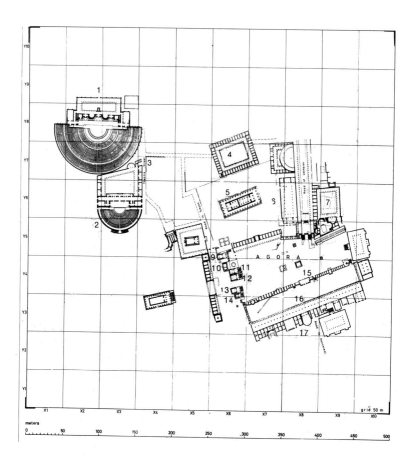

Corinth: Plan of the Agora
Source: Plan D-AGC 619A by the Athens Center of Ekistics

1 Theater
2 Odeion
3 Sanctuary of Athena Chalinitis
4 North Market
5 Temple of Apollo
6 North Basilica
7 Sanctuary of Apollo
8 Fountain House (Peirene)
9 Temple D — Hermes?

10 Temple K — Apollo Klarios?
11 Temple J — Poseidon?
12 Temple H — Herakles Commodus?
13 Temple G — Pantheon?
14 Temple F — Venus Fortuna?
15 Bema
16 South Stoa
17 Bouleuterion

by sea was easier, and it is likely that St. Paul sailed from Piraeus between the islands of Salamis and Aegina to the harbor of Cenchreae on the eastern shore of the Isthmus of Corinth. The distance from Cenchreae to Corinth is about 9 kilometers, and would have taken the Apostle two or three hours to walk. Ahead of him rose Acrocorinth, 571 meters above sea level, and at its base lay Corinth. Entering the city through the Cenchreae gate, the Apostle would have passed through the suburb of Craneum, with its cypress grove, gymnasium, and sanctuaries of Bellerophon and Aphrodite, and it is likely that the suburb's name would have brought to his mind the Craneion, or Golgotha — the place of the skull — outside the walls of Jerusalem where his Lord had been crucified (John 19:17).

Corinth in the days of St. Paul was an altogether different city from Athens. It was not a Greek provincial town but the capital of a Roman province, a busy metropolis which flourished as a commercial center because of its advantageous geographical location. It had been destroyed in 146 B.C. by Lucius Mummius and had lain in ruins until it was rebuilt by Julius Caesar in 44 B.C. and became known as Laus Julia Corinthiensis. Whereas Athens somehow retained its Hellenic image, in Corinth Greeks, Jews, and Orientals mixed with the Roman military colonists.

One of the first writers to provide us with a description of the new Roman colony is the Greek geographer Strabo of Amasia in Pontus, who lived in the first century B.C. Among other things he tells us that

> Corinth is called wealthy because of its commerce, since it lies at the Isthmus and controls two harbours, one of which is near Asia, and the other near Italy . . . but further profits also accrued to the people afterwards, for the celebration of the Isthmian Games brought in crowds . . . The sanctuary of Aphrodite was so wealthy that it possessed as slaves of the temple more than one thousand courtesans, who were dedicated to the goddess both by men and women. And so by reason of them, the city was thronged and enriched for the sailors spent their money easily, and on that account the proverb says: "Not for every man is the voyage to Corinth."

When the colonists arrived in 44 B.C., they restored the worship of most of the ancient gods. In the center of the city stood the archaic temple to Apollo which, even in St. Paul's day, must have been one of the most conspicuous monuments. The temple of Athena Chalinitis (The Bridler) was on the north slope, while in the agora there were a shrine and fountain dedicated to Poseidon. Several sanctuaries to Apollo were within the city, and in the agora there were temples dedicated to Herakles, Poseidon, Apollo, and Hermes. For their own cults the colonists built a temple to Venus-Fortuna and next to it a temple dedicated to "All the Gods" (the Pantheon), at the western end of the agora. Shortly before St. Paul's time the agora had been divided into two levels. The lower agora was used mainly for commercial purposes and the upper agora was used for administrative, political, and religious functions.

Far from the agora at the northern edge of the ancient city there stood the famous temple dedicated to Asklepios, the god of healing, and his daughter Hygieia. Patients from near and far used to come to Corinth for treatment. More famous still was the temple of Aphrodite, located on the topmost peak of Acrocorinth, whose female servants gave Corinth its reputation for immortality to which St. Paul alluded repeatedly (I Cor. 6:9-20, II Cor. 12:20-21). According to Pausanias, "Her image represents the goddess armed, and there are images of the Sun, and of Love, the latter bearing a bow." The temple of Aphrodite which existed in St. Paul's time was a Doric temple built in the 4th or 5th century B.C. It was small, approximately 10 by 16 meters, and only traces of it remain today.

Corinth commanded the land route over the narrow isthmus connecting the southern and central parts of Greece. The harbor of Lechaion on the Gulf of Corinth afforded sea communications with the west, as did the harbor of Cenchreae to the Aegean Sea and the east. In St. Paul's time ships crossing the isthmus were

Corinth: Temple of Apollo and Acrocorinth

dragged overland on rollers or waggons. The Corinth canal, although considered by Alexander the Great, Julius Caesar, and Caligula, and begun by the engineers of Nero, was not actually cut until the latter part of the 19th century.

We are fortunate in having two extra-scriptural sources of information at our disposal which help us date the Apostle's ministry in Corinth. In the Acts of the Apostles we are informed that when St. Paul came to Corinth he met with a Jew called Aquila, a native of Pontus, and his wife Priscilla, who had recently arrived from Rome. Apparently St. Paul's arrival in Corinth almost coincided with that of Aquila and Priscilla, and the Claudian decree expelling the Jews from Rome had been promulgated a short time before that. This was not the first time that the Romans had taken measures against the Jews in their capital. Tiberius (14-37 A.D.) deported the able-bodied Jews to Sardinia and ordered the rest to leave the city. In the beginning of the reign of Claudius the Jews enjoyed a good deal of freedom, yet, after some time, Claudius seemed to have found it necessary to expel the Jews again from Rome. As the Roman historian Suetonius puts it in his *Life of Claudius* "The Jews, who by the instigation of one Chrestos were evermore tumultuous, he banished from Rome" and, according to the 5th century Spanish historian Paulus Orosius, this expulsion occurred in the ninth year of the reign of Claudius. The ninth year of Claudius's reign extended from January 25th, 49 to January 24th, 50. It is within this period, therefore, that we should place the arrival of Aquila and Priscilla in Corinth.

An additional date pertaining to the Apostle's stay in Corinth is supplied by some fragments of an inscription cut in a limestone slab discovered in Delphi in the latter part of the last century. They are of great help for the dating of St. Paul's stay in Corinth, for the text of the inscription refers to Gallio's proconsulship in Achaia (Acts 18:12). Gallio, the brother of the Roman philosopher Seneca, was proconsul during at least part of St. Paul's stay in the city.

St. Luke informs us that St. Paul had settled down in Corinth for eighteen months and taught God's message. Then, while Gallio was proconsul of Achaia, the Jews banded together to attack the Apostle and they took him to court. The reconstructed text of the slab states among other things that

> Tiberius Claudius Caesar Augustus Germanicus, pontifex maximus, in the 12th year of his tribunal power, acclaimed emperor for the 26th time. . . sends greetings to the city of Delphi...but with regard to the present stories and those disputes of the citizens of which a report has been made by Lucius Junius Gallio, my friend a proconsul of Achaia. . .

Though fascinating from an historical point of view, this is not the place to discuss the content of this imperial message beyond our particular interest in the date of Gallio's stay in Achaia. The 12th tribunal year of the emperor extended from January 25th, 52 to January 24th, 53. From various contemporary sources we know that the 23rd to the 27th acclamations occurred in the interval between January 25th, 51 and August 1st, 52. These imperial acclamations were in response to victories achieved either by the emperor or one of his officers. There is good reason to believe that the 26th acclamation occurred during the first six months of the year 52, the time during which Claudius wrote his message to the people in Delphi. The text of the above mentioned inscription presupposes, however, that Gallio had stayed in Achaia for some time. His appointment to Achaia, therefore, may well have taken place in the spring of 51, since government officials serving the provinces normally held office for only one year and were transferred in the spring. Accordingly, the attack of the Corinthian Jews on the Apostle occurred at the earliest in the spring of 51 and at the latest in the spring of 52. St. Luke speaks of St. Paul's ministry in Corinth as lasting eighteen months. Since the earliest date of the Apostle's appearance before the proconsul is the spring of 51, the Apostle then could not have arrived in Corinth before the first days of the year 50.

Here he met with Priscilla and Aquila, the two refugees from Rome, who worked at the same craft as the Apostle. The trade at which they labored was the manufacture of tents, the demand for which must have been continual. Most of the cloth for these tents was made from goat hair, and the tents were known as *cilicium,* after the province of Cilicia of which the Apostle was a native. We do not know whether Priscilla and Aquila were already Christians when they met St. Paul. They may have been converted in Rome, although there is no evidence to this effect. It is, of course, impossible to determine the exact location of Priscilla and Aquila's shop, where the Apostle worked with his hands, as he later reminded the Corinthians (I Cor. 4:12), but

Ken Shapiro

Corinth: St. Aquila on the iconostasis in the Cathedral of St. Paul it was probably located not far from the point where the Lechaion Road led into the agora. Socket holes for tent awnings have been found in the lower agora and it is quite possible that St. Paul and his friends, Aquila and Priscilla, being tent makers, made some of the tents used here.

Priscilla and Aquila, who probably sailed from Ostia or Puteoli, Rome's two ports, would have disembarked at Lechaion, Corinth's western port. Although today the bay is very shallow, the outline of the ancient harbor can still be seen.

Lechaion: Marble capital from the Basilica of St. Leonidas and the Seven Virgins(?)

Recent excavations in Lechaion have uncovered the ruins of one of the largest Byzantine churches in Greece (184×45 meters). This monumental basilica is thought to have been a martyrium dedicated to St. Leonidas and the Seven Virgins, Chariessa, Galene, Nike, Kallida, Nunechia, Basilissa, and Theodora who, on Easter Monday 250, suffered martyrdom by drowning at Troezen, southeast of Corinth. The basilica was built in the 5th century and enlarged during the reign of Justin (518-527) just a few years before it was destroyed by an earthquake.

PREACHING

And he argued in the synagogue every' sabbath, and persuaded Jews and Greeks.
And when they opposed and reviled him, he shook out his garments and said to them, "Your blood be upon your heads! I am innocent. From now on I will go to the Gentiles."

Acts 18:4, 6

Since the Apostle would not work on the Sabbath, he would take the opportunity and preach in the local synagogue, where he addressed both Jews and Greeks, pointing out to them that the Old Testament promise had been fulfilled in Jesus Christ. This very heart of the Christian message, that Jesus was the Christ, became the *casus belli* for the local Jews.

When Silas and Timothy arrived from Macedonia, Paul was occupied with preaching, testifying to the Jews that the Christ was Jesus.

Acts 18:5

Lechaion: Ruins of the Basilica of St. Leonidas and the Seven Virgins(?)

71

Corinth: Synagogue inscription, in the Archaeological Museum

Ken Shapiro

The arrival in Corinth of Silas and Timothy, who had come from Macedonia, was one of the most significant interruptions in the Corinthian ministry of the Apostle, because their news from the Christians in Thessalonica prompted the Apostle to compose the first document of the New Testament, the First Letter to the Thessalonians. The Apostle's difficulties in Corinth, especially the opposition which he encountered from the Jewish section of the population, are reflected in this first letter (I Thess. 2:15-16).

We do not know how long the Apostle taught in the synagogue in Corinth. Furthermore, no exact information as to the location of the synagogue in Corinth is so far available, although an interesting inscription was found at the foot of the steps of the gateway leading into the agora from the Lechaion Road. On a long heavy block, apparently the upper lintel of a doorway, are carved seven letters which are part of an inscription which translates "Synagogue of the Jews." The letters read: [ΣΥΝΑ]ΓΩΓΗ ΕΒΡ [ΑΙΩΝ]. The careless style of the lettering, however, indicates that the inscription, and presumably also the synagogue to which it belonged, should be assigned to a later period, probably the 5th century.

In addition to this inscription, the American archaeologists excavating in Corinth discovered a marble impost on which is carved a design including three seven branched candlesticks (menorah) with palm leaves. This impost, which has been assigned to the 5th century, was actually found in the theater. Unfortunately, the location of neither of these two finds indicate the location of the synagogue in Corinth.

> And he left there and went to the house of a man named Titius Justus, a worshiper of God; his house was next door to the synagogue. Crispus, the ruler of the synagogue, believed in the Lord, together with all his household; and many of the Corinthians hearing Paul believed and were baptized. And the Lord said to Paul one night in a vision, "Do not be afraid, but speak and do not be silent; for I am with you, and no man shall attack you to harm you; for I

Ken Shapiro

Corinth: Marble impost with three menorahs, in the Archaeological Museum

have many people in this city." And he stayed a year and six months, teaching the word of God among them.

Acts 18:7-11

After the Apostle was evicted from the synagogue, he turned again to the Gentiles. This had happened before and yet, in each new city, he tried to preach to his own people first. Fortunately, a proselyte by the name of Titius Justus opened his door to the Apostle, and the house of Justus, next door to the synagogue, became the church in Corinth.

There are few congregations of the apostolic period of which we know more details than the church in Corinth. Names of individuals and whole families are mentioned either in the Acts or in St. Paul's correspondence. It certainly was no overstatement when we read that "many of the Corinthians hearing believed and were baptized." Some of the earliest converts were members of the family of Stephanas; then there was Gaius, with whom St. Paul found a home on his next visit (I Cor. 1:14, Rom 16:23). There were also "Chloe's people," whoever they were, and Quartus, Fortunatus, and Tertius. In addition to these Roman colonists were three Jews, Lucius, Jason, and Sosipater. Apparently, the majority of the people who were converted to the Gospel of Jesus Christ in Corinth were simple people. They were not philosophers, the noble, or the powerful (I Cor. 1:26), but rather the ignorant of this world, elected to confound the wise; the weak, who were called to confound the strong.

There was, however, at least one exception to this rule. Among the most interesting discoveries at Corinth is an inscribed block used in an ancient repair of a pavement in the little ancient square at the northern end of the street leading past the theater. The letters are deeply hollowed out and were once filled with bronze and fastened in place with lead. They read

ERASTVS PRO AEDILITATE
S P STRAVIT

that is,

ERASTUS PRO AEDILITATE SUA PECUNIA STRAVIT

74

Corinth: Erastus pavement inscription

Ken Shapiro

"Erastus, in return for his aedilship, laid the pavement at his own expense." This pavement was in existence when St. Paul visited the city of Corinth. In his letter of recommendation for Phoebe, a deaconess of the church of Cenchreae, the Apostle included "Erastus the city treasurer" (Rom. 16:23) in a list of people sending greetings to the sister congregation. The Greek word *oikonomos,* which appears in the original text, is the equivalent of the Latin *aedilis.* A Roman *aedilis* of a city like Corinth would normally have been a man of great influence and wealth, and so we may assume that there was at least one member of the political elite in the Corinthian congregation.

In general, the Gentile population was more receptive to the Apostle's message than the Jews, but here also we find a notable exception. Crispus, the ruler of the synagogue, together with his family, joined the newly founded church. The conversion of Crispus must have made a lasting impression upon the Jewish community, in which opposition increased as the Christian community grew.

GALLIO

> But when Gallio was proconsul of Achaia, the Jews made a united attack upon Paul and brought him before the tribunal, saying, "This man is persuading men to worship God contrary to the law." But when Paul was about to open his mouth, Gallio said to the Jews, "If it were a matter of wrongdoing or vicious crime, I should have reason to bear with you, O Jews; but since it is a matter of questions about words and names and your own law, see to it yourselves; I refuse to be a judge of these things." And he drove them from the tribunal. And they all seized Sosthenes, the ruler of the synagogue, and beat him in front of the tribunal. But Gallio paid no attention to this.

> Acts 18:12-17

As we have mentioned, the proconsul Gallio was the brother of the famous Roman philosopher Annaeus Seneca, the tutor of Nero. He had been adopted by his father's friend, Junius Gallio, the great rhetorician, and had taken on his name. Annaeus Seneca thought highly of his brother. He referred in his writings to Gallio's pleasant character and disposition, and he dedicated two of his works, *De Ira* and *De Vita Beata,* to him. Gallio's manner of dealing with the uproar in Corinth justifies the high repute in which he was held. His refusal to get involved in a quarrel which did not affect the state demonstrated a great deal of administrative wisdom. Pliny informs us that Gallio contracted a serious illness after his proconsulship, and that he undertook a sea journey to cure his ailments.

The principal spokesman for the Jews against St. Paul seems

to have been a certain Sosthenes, the leader of the synagogue, who was the successor to Crispus or, perhaps, the leader of another synagogue. Undoubtedly, this Sosthenes is not the "brother" of the same name mentioned in I Cor. 1:1. At any rate, the Apostle did not even have to state his case, for the proconsul spoke before him and this settled the issue. The Jews were removed from the court and Sosthenes was beaten by the crowd in front of the courthouse.

After this incident St. Paul was no longer molested by the Jews and he continued his work in spreading the Gospel among the Corinthians. The assurance communicated to him in his vision was fulfilled:

> Do not be afraid, but speak and do not be silent; for I am with you, and no man shall attack you to harm you; for I have many people in this city.
>
> Acts 18:9

Tradition, supported by the judgment of some archaeologists, has identified the site where the Apostle was brought before Gallio with the bema. Like the rostra in the forum in Rome, the tribune in Corinth, called in Greek a *bema,* faced the agora and was flanked by central shops on either side. This bema was used by officials for appearances before the public, gathered in the lower section of the agora. In the days of the Apostle this bema must have been an impressive structure. The entrance was from the rear through three openings separated by massive marble piers. In the 10th century a church with three apses was built here, perhaps on the ruins of an earlier, smaller church. Many Christian graves were cut in the hard rubble which forms the core of the bema.

The question before us now, however, is whether this bema could have been the site where the Apostle stood in front of Gallio. The Lukan account mentions no specific location. Professor Erich Dinkler has convincingly pointed out that it is most unlikely that Gallio would have convened a court in such a public place, and we know from similar cases that the Roman provincial courts usually were convened in a basilica or in the prae-

torium. A new city like Corinth may even have held its court in one of the basilicas, probably the northern one, which is parallel to the Lechaion Road. This basilica, which dates from the first century B.C., presumably had a tribunal at its northern end, although no traces of it remain. Was St. Paul, perhaps, taken to this site?

There is no church commemorating St. Paul's ministry in Old Corinth, but there is a large cruciform cathedral named after the Apostle in New Corinth. The foundation stone of this cathedral was laid in 1934 by the Metropolitan Damaskinos who later became Archbishop of Athens and All Greece. Every year on June 29th a vesper service (hesperinos) is conducted by the Metropolitan of Corinth at the traditional bema in the ruins of Old Corinth, during which one of the bishops or a professor of the theological faculties delivers the memorial sermon. In addition, on every February 13th a vesper service is celebrated in honor of St. Paul's co-workers in Corinth, the saints Aquila and Priscilla. Metropolitan Panteleimon of Corinth hopes to build an additional chapel in honor of St. Paul in connection with an old people's home in the city. On Apostle Paul Street opposite the Cathedral of St. Paul is an ecclesiastical museum with a rich collection of 17th to 19th century icons and liturgical objects, well worth a visit.

It is not unreasonable to speculate that the Apostle established other Christian congregations during his stay in Corinth, since his Second Letter to the Corinthians is also addressed to "The saints who are in the whole of Achaia." Neither St. Paul's letters nor the Acts of the Apostles, however, mention any journey from the Corinth area to preach the Gospel elsewhere in Achaia, and any such visits to the Peloponnesos or the Greek islands must be considered hypothetical. Nevertheless, during his stay

Corinth: Bema

Corinth: Marble funerary slab from the Byzantine church on the Bema

Ken Shapiro

in Corinth, St. Paul may have visited the Jewish communities in Argos in the Peloponnessos and those on the islands of Aegina and Delos, each of which maintained a synagogue, for we know that wherever St. Paul went he first addressed the Jews in the synagogue. The least likely of these visits would have been to Argos, for we know of its synagogue only from

Philo and the journey would have been a long one over land. A journey to the islands of Aegina and Delos, however, would have been made by boat, and the archaeological evidence of synagogues on these islands during St. Paul's time suggests at least the possibility of Pauline visits.

The synagogue on Aegina was near the harbor. Fourth century remains of a hall, an apse in the eastern wall, and a mosaic floor have been found built on the ruins of an earlier synagogue. The mosaic consists of geometric designs giving the impression of a carpet and containing a Greek inscription reading "I, Theodoros, the archisynagogos, who functioned for four years, built this synagogue from its foundations. Revenues amounted to 85 pieces of gold (dinars) and offerings unto God of 105 pieces of gold." The mosaic has been moved to the archaeological site of the Hill of Kolona, where it may be seen just inside the entrance. The earlier synagogue on which these 4th century remains were built would have been standing at the time of the Apostle's ministry in Corinth.

Delos, the smallest of the Cyclades Islands, became, because of its central position, a major trading center for the eastern

Ken Shapiro

Aegina: Synagogue mosaic inscription

Corinth: The cathedral of St. Paul in the modern city

Ken Shapiro

Mediterranean during the centuries immediately preceding the Christian era, and many Jews were attracted to it. A Jewish community on Delos is mentioned in I Macc. 1:15, 23 and the Jewish historian Josephus has preserved two official documents referring to this community. A synagogue in the northeast of the island, east of the stadium and near the shore, has been excavated by the French Archaeological Institute in Athens. The French archaeologists assign the building to the end of the 2nd century B.C., making it one of the oldest synagogues found.

THE ISTHMIAN GAMES

It is of little importance for our discussion whether we accept the theory of Professor Oscar Broneer that St. Paul came to Corinth because of the Isthmian Games, or whether the Apostle merely visited the Isthmian Games during his first stay in the city. That he was acquainted with the Games is evident from the literary images he employs:

> Do you not know that in a race all the runners compete, but only one receives the prize? So run that you may obtain it. Every athlete exercises self-control in all things. They do it to receive a perishable wreath, but we an imperishable. Well, I do not run aimlessly, I do not box as one beating the air; but I pommel my body and subdue it, lest after preaching to others I myself should be disqualified.
>
> I Cor. 9:24-27.

In using these images the Apostle quite rightly assumed that every Corinthian was thoroughly familiar with them. But St. Paul was not an athlete, and so the images are somehow mixed up. He began with the foot race, in which there is only one winner, but in the church, of course all could win the prize. Then he shifted from the second to the first person, for he was thinking specifically of his own struggle and, after referring again to the runner, he switched over to the boxer. C.T. Craig sums up his commentary to this passage by saying:

> Out of this jumble of figures comes one clear picture — the earnestness of the Apostle, who, though he was giving his life for the Gospel, realized that he was still untrue to his demands. The strong must take care on their own account.

The Panhellenic festival known as the Isthmian Games was held every two years in honor of Poseidon, god of the sea, and the boy-god Palaimon. It attracted many delegates, athletes, visitors, and merchants to Isthmia, approximately 10 kilometers east of Old Corinth near the eastern end of the modern canal.

The festival offered unusual opportunities for the Apostle to preach the Gospel, and perhaps to also maintain his contacts with the Christian communities in Macedonia and Asia Minor. Professionally, St. Paul would also have profited from the Games, when large numbers of tents would be needed to shelter the many visitors.

In April or May of the year 51, St. Paul may have set out for the Isthmian sanctuary, perhaps accompanied by Timothy, Silas, Priscilla, Aquila, and even by some of his new converts such as Crispus and Stephanas. They would have been able easily to make the trip in one day. "On entering the sanctuary of the god,"

Corinth: Mosaic of victorious athlete crowned with perishable wreath before the goddess Eutychia

Pausanias wrote, there were "on one side statues of athletes who have been victorious in the Isthmian Games, and on the other side a row of pine trees." In addition to the sanctuary were the Temple of Poseidon, the theater, on a hillside sloping towards the north, and the so-called Later Stadium, which is now occupied by a flourishing grove of citrus trees.

In the Southern Stoa in Old Corinth, the archaeologists of the American School of Classical Studies discovered a mosaic floor which may have adorned the office of the director of the Isthmian Games. The mosaic is well preserved and shows a victorious athlete with a palm branch in his hand and a crown of withered celery. He is standing in front of the goddess of good fortune, Eutychia, to whom he renders thanks for his success.

The Isthmian crown, which St. Paul refers to in his letter as "a perishable wreath," was the principal reward presented at the games. The crowns presented at the Panhellenic festivals of Olympia and Pythia were made of wild olive and laurel, respectively. The crowns for the festivals of Nemea and Isthmia were of wild celery. The Isthmian crown, however, was not made of fresh, but of withered wild celery, which explains the Apostle's image of "the perishable wreath."

DEPARTURE FROM CENCHREAE

> After this Paul stayed many days longer, and then took leave of the brethren and sailed for Syria, and with him Priscilla and Aquila. At Cenchreae he cut his hair, for he had a vow.
>
> Acts 18:18

The time had come for the Apostle to move on. It must have been a very touching farewell. St. Paul had been singularly successful and had made many friends and converts in this city and, as we shall see, Corinth and the Corinthians remained in his mind for many years to come. Leaving the city, he would have traveled several miles across the Isthmian plain to the eastern

Corinthian coin minted during the reign of Antoninus Pius showing the harbor of Cenchraea

harbor of Cenchreae, where he embarked for Ephesus.

Cenchreae, the eastern port of Corinth, must have been a town of some magnitude in the days of St. Paul. Pausanias informs us that at Cenchreae

> there is a temple of Aphrodite and beyond the temple there is a bronze image of Poseidon on the mole that runs into the sea. At the other extremity of the harbor are sanctuaries of Aesculapius and Isis.

In the 10th book of *The Golden Ass,* the 2nd century A.D. Platonic philosopher, Lucius Apuleius, described Cenchreae as "the most famous town of all the Corinthians, bordering upon the seas called Aegean and Saronic. There is a great and mighty haven frequented with the ships of many sundry nations." The remains of Cenchreae's ancient moles and warehouses have been studied by American underwater archaeologists under

Cenchreae: Ruins of Byzantine church

the direction of Robert Scranton. The ruins of a Christian church with a single apse and nave are on the road leading to the warehouses and the western mole. In the 6th century the harbor was abandoned, though a small community of Christians survived for several more centuries. The whole coastline must have sunk several feet during the last fourteen hundred years.

The reference "he cut his hair" has led to a geat deal of speculation as to whether this pertained to Aquila or St. Paul. Grammatically, it might be Aquila who is meant, but if so it seems unlikely that St. Luke would have considered the incident worth recording. It is much more probable that the reference is to St. Paul. The vow would be a Nazarite vow:

> All the days of his vow of separation no razor shall come upon his head; until the time is completed for which he separates himself to the Lord, he shall be holy; he shall let the locks of hair of his head grow long.
>
> Numbers 6:5

The cutting of hair and the burning of it as a sacrifice (Num. 6:18), marked the completion of the vow. Before setting sail for Palestine, then, the Apostle was redeeming such a vow. All we can say is that, apparently, in spite of his strong antinomian pronouncements, St. Paul still adhered to certain Jewish rituals. This is also evident from his visit to the temple and his purification preceding it (Acts 21:26).

ST. PAUL WRITES TO THE CORINTHIANS

Approximately two years passed and the Apostle seems to have been well established in Ephesus when he received word from Chloe's people who arrived from Corinth. The church in Corinth was in trouble. The congregation was splitting into rival groups clustered about their favorite teachers (I Cor. 1:10-4:21), one of whom was Apollos, the eloquent Alexandrian preacher. Some members of the Corinthian congregation had come to consider St. Paul inferior to St. Peter who, after all, had seen Jesus Christ in the flesh. But even more serious problems were reported by Chloe's people. There were cases of immorality and one man had married his widowed stepmother. Moreover, degeneration in the manner in which the Lord's Supper was observed was cause for serious alarm.

Ken Shapiro

Corinth: St. Apollos on the iconostasis in the Cathedral of St. Paul

When you meet together, it is not the Lord's supper that you eat. For in eating, each one goes ahead with his own meal, and one is hungry and another is drunk. What! Do you not have houses to eat and drink in? Or do you despise the church of God and humiliate those who have nothing? What shall I say to you? Shall I commend you in this? No, I will not.

I Cor. 11:20-22

The problem of where they could purchase their meat bothered many Corinthian Christians, since the best meat was sold at the markets connected with the pagan temples. Was it appropriate for Christians to eat meat which had been offered to idols? Some members of the congregation saw no problem in eating sacrificial meat, but others had great misgivings about it, pointing out that this made the Christians supporters of heathen cults.

Several years ago the American archaeologists investigating the long stoa in the southwest of the agora discovered what could have been the Corinthian *macellum*, or meat market. In the southern half of the stoa they found 33 shops, each with

Drawing of inscription found on door jamb, Corinth

a storeroom in the rear and a well. The wells probably were used as cold storage areas, indicating that perishable food was either kept or sold here. On a block which had been used as a door jamb they also found the faint inscription ΛΟΥΚΙΟC ΛΑΝ(Ι)ΟC, or Lucius the butcher, *lanios,* the Latin word for butcher, being written in Greek letters. Perhaps this is a hint that the Corinthian meat market mentioned by St. Paul in I Cor. 10:25 was in the southwestern part of the agora, although it has also been thought that these shops were taverns.

The Corinthian agora provided an additional metaphor for the Apostle. In the Letter to the Romans, which he wrote during his last visit to Corinth, he used the analogy of the potter's right over clay to explain that God's choice, even if arbitrary, is never unjust (Rom. 9:19-21). The ruins of many potters' workshops and large quantities of vases have been uncovered near Corinth's western city wall. St. Paul may have had this potters' quarter in mind when he wrote, "Has the potter no right over the clay, to make of the same lump one vessel for beauty and another for material use?"

The Corinthian church was a troubled community. How were the members to conduct themselves in church? Should the women wear or not wear veils? Should the men have long or short hair? What about those who felt they were moved by the spirit and expressed themselves in tongues? All of these manifold problems required a reply, and St. Paul's First Letter to the Corinthians is his attempt to provide guidelines and answers. Like a responsible shepherd, he dealt with each item on the list as reported by Chloe's people.

There is some evidence that, in addition to the report by Chloe's people, St. Paul was kept informed by others of what was going on in the Corinthian congregation. Visitors from Corinth must have been quite frequent in Ephesus, which was no more than a couple of days by sail from Corinth. It is difficult, however, for us to know the extent of the correspondence between the Apostle and the Corinthian church. In I Cor. 5:9, St. Paul speaks of a letter in which he admonished the Corinthian Christians not to associate with immoral people. Probably this was a short letter, and it may well be preserved in part as II

Cor. 6:14 - 7:1. It seems that in reply to this particular letter, the Corinthians asked further questions which were then answered by St. Paul in I Cor. 7.

Before turning to the Apostle's replies, we should remember that St. Paul held certain basic assumptions. For example, he shared with many other Christians of his age certain views pertaining to the immediate end of the world; views which undoubtedly affected many of his answers. Furthermore, most of his replies were in response to specific issues. Despite the situational nature of his correspondence, however, throughout it runs a consistent thread of profound Christian thought, which provides theological and soteriological direction.

On the issue of Corinthian sectarianism, St. Paul issued as strong a condemnation as he could:

> I appeal to you, brethren, by the name of our Lord Jesus Christ, that all of you agree and that there be no dissensions among you, but that you be united in the same mind and the same judgment.
>
> I Cor. 1:10

> What do you wish? Shall I come to you with a rod, or with love in a spirit of gentleness?
>
> I Cor. 4:21

He dealt sternly with the case of the man who had married his widowed stepmother by asking the Corinthians to excommunicate him:

> When you are assembled, and my spirit is present, with the power of our Lord Jesus, you are to deliver this man to Satan for the destruction of the flesh, that his spirit may be saved in the day of the Lord Jesus.
>
> I Cor. 5:4

In I Corinthians 5 and 6 St. Paul takes up the issue of immorality in Corinth, insisting upon the Christian duty of purity. There was every reason for the Apostle to be concerned. After all, already in the days of Aristophanes in the 5th century B.C., to be called a Corinthian was to be called immoral. A 4th century B.C. inscription reading "belonging to the girls" was found on a block used in the earliest construction of the theater. The inscription may have designated a section of the theater reserved for "the girls," who probably were the notorious temple prostitutes of Aphrodite, since respectable women did not patronize the theater.

> Do not be deceived; neither the immoral, nor idolaters, nor adulterers, nor homosexuals, nor thieves, nor the greedy, nor drunkards, nor revilers, nor robbers will inherit the kingdom of God.
>
> I Cor. 6:9b-10

Apparently the Corinthians had written the Apostle for advice on the whole issue of marriage and sex, to which I Cor. chapter 7 is his reply heavily colored by his eschatological expectations. The Lord is at hand and, therefore, let the unmarried remain chaste. It is not a sin, certainly, to get married but, after all, unmarried men and women are more free to do the Lord's work. A Christian married to a non-Christian wife who is willing to live with him should not divorce her, and the same pertains to a Christian woman married to a pagan man.

It was not particularly strange that the observance of the Lord's Supper should have degenerated. The Dionysiac and Orphic mysteries provided all kinds of excitement at their sacramental meals, which included eating the flesh and drinking the blood of a kid or a bull identified with a god. St. Paul dealt with this matter with considerable sternness. He repeated, evidently from an oral gospel familiar to the Corinthians in its Greek form, the oldest account of the Last Supper, and admonished them to make every observance of it an occasion of serious self examination (I Cor. 11:17-34).

The issue of special spiritual endowments, particularly the disturbing matter of ecstatic speaking, was a difficult problem among the Corinthian Christians. The Apostle hesitated to offend anyone, yet he admonished his brothers not to be childish

(I Cor. 14:20) in their thinking. All things should be for edification.

> If any speak in a tongue, let there be only two or at most three, and each in turn; and let one interpret. But if there is no one to interpret, let each of them keep silence in church and speak to himself and to God.
>
> I Cor. 14:27-28

St. Paul took the opportunity to stress the importance of the Christian's belief in the resurrection.

> If Christ has not been raised, then our preaching is in vain and your faith is in vain. We are even found to be misrepresenting God, because we testified of God that he raised Christ.
>
> I Cor. 15:14-15

The letter draws to a close with several business and personal matters, greetings to some of the leaders of the church, and a promise to visit the Christians in Corinth.

> I will visit you after passing through Macedonia, . . . and perhaps I will stay with you or even spend the winter, so that you may speed me on my journey, wherever I go.
>
> I Cor. 16:5-6

ST. PAUL'S RETURN VISITS

Although the Apostle stayed in Ephesus for approximately two and a half years, he kept the Corinthian congregation in his mind. In the spring of 55 he had sent his first letter to them, which is mentioned in I Cor. 5:9. Shortly afterwards he received a reply from the Corinthians as referred to in I Cor. 7:1. He then commissioned Timothy to take his second letter to the Corinthians, which is now known as the First Letter of Paul to the Corinthians. Sometime later the Apostle sent another letter, which is incorporated in II Cor. 2:14 - 7:4.

94

It must have been approximately autumn in the year 55 when St. Paul made a brief visit to Corinth. St. Luke did not mention it in the Acts, but numerous references in St. Paul's own writings imply a visit which, apparently, was painful. Trouble had broken out again in Corinth. Certain Jewish Christians had arrived in the city carrying letters of recommendation (II Cor. 3) and claiming the right to exercise authoritative leadership in the church. St. Paul sailed from Ephesus directly to Cenchreae, the eastern port of Corinth, to deal summarily with his opponents, but he neither settled the disputes nor expelled the intruders. His authority had been severely shaken. With a harsh warning, to which he referred before his third visit, he left Corinth and returned to Ephesus.

> I warned those who sinned before and all the others, and I warn them now while absent, as I did when present on my second visit, that if I come again I will not spare them.
>
> II Cor. 13:2

The Apostle addressed a fourth letter to the Corinthians after his unsuccessful visit. Conveyed by Titus, this letter is found in II Cor. 10-13.

After dispatching Titus to Corinth, St. Paul visited Macedonia as recorded by St. Luke (Acts 20:1-2). Somewhere in Macedonia, probably in Philippi, he met with Titus, who brought heartening news about Corinth (II Cor. 7:6-7). The church had repudiated the arrogant intruders and all seemed well under control.

St. Paul could now move on to Corinth without fear of trouble or repudiation, but he wanted the collection of the Corinthians for the Jerusalem Church to be prepared before he arrived.

> Now it is superfluous for me to write to you about the offering for the saints, for I know your readiness, of which I boast about you to the people of Macedonia, saying that Achaia has been ready since last year; and your zeal has stirred up most of them.
>
> II Cor. 9:1-3

Apparently the Corinthians had begun the work but, to avoid any embarrassment to them and to himself, St. Paul sent messengers ahead to insure that everything was in order.

> So I thought it necessary to urge the brethren to go on to you before me, and arrange in advance for this gift you have promised, so that it may be ready not as an exaction but as a willing gift.
>
> II Cor. 9:5

St. Paul stayed in Macedonia for some time, completing the collection there, before he proceeded to Corinth.

About St. Paul's third visit to Corinth, during the winter months of 55 and 56, we know almost nothing more than that he remained for three months. During this last stay in Corinth the Apostle composed his letter to the Romans, the most important Christian theological treatise ever written. The West was calling him; he wanted to visit the church in Rome. This time in Corinth he was undisturbed by intrigues and difficulties, and the Corinthians must have provided a spiritual climate that enabled him to write. We feel that the final chapter of this letter, Romans 16, was in fact addressed to the church in Ephesus, and carried there by Phoebe, the deaconess of the church in Cenchreae (Rom. 16:1).

After three months, St. Paul prepared to return to Syria. He had intended to embark from Cenchreae when he discovered a plot directed against him by the Jews. We do not know the nature of the plot. Was it an attempt to assassinate the Apostle on the high seas? What were the reasons? Was it a matter of personal animosity, a reflection of the troubles which he had in Corinth on a previous occasion? Or was it that he was carrying the collection? At any rate, instead of taking a ship he went by land to Macedonia. The land journey had the additional advantage that it enabled him to collect the company of delegates who were to join him on his journey to Jerusalem.

THE APOSTOLIC CHURCH IN CORINTH

Did St. Paul address additional letters to the Corinthians which did not find their way into the canon of the New Testament? The lack of a text for the letter mentioned in I Cor. 5:9 led to apocryphal writings. From the middle of the 2nd century on, a letter from the elders of the church in Corinth to St. Paul and his reply were circulated in the Syrian (Edessene) Church. According to the Church Father Tertullian (155-222 A.D.), this correspondence was written by a Christian elder in Asia in approximately 160 A.D. It lost its canonical status in the early 5th century, when the Syrian Church came under the influence of the Greek Church, but it was included in the Armenian New Testament for several more centuries.

The letter to St. Paul complains of the arrival of false teachers who threaten the faith "for we have never heard such words from thee nor from the other apostles." The letter asks the Apostle "either to come to us or write to us, for we believe, according as it hath been revealed to Theonoë, that the Lord hath delivered thee out of the hands of the lawless one." The replying letter from the Apostle responds to each charge made by the false teachers about the authority of the Old Testament prophets, the question of the omnipotence of God, the doctrine of the resurrection of the flesh, the creation of man, and the incarnation of God in Jesus Christ. Despite the apocryphal nature of these letters, the correspondence of the elders with the Apostle is evidence of the importance of the Corinthian congregation in the early Church.

The importance of the early church in Corinth is well attested by St. Clement's Letter to the Corinthians, written in approximately 96 A.D. As in the days of St. Paul, the Corinthian church labored with the problem of disunity which came to the attention of the bishop of Rome. St. Clement's Letter to the Corinthians is the earliest source which speaks of St. Paul's teaching "righteousness in the whole world and having reached the farthest bounds of the West," probably Spain, and his martyrdom.

According to tradition, the first leaders of the church in

Corinth were Apollos (Acts 18:24, I Cor. 1:12, 3:4-6, 4:6), Silas (Acts 15:22-18:5), and Sosthenes (Acts 18:17, I Cor. 1:1). In the 2nd century the church was led by Apollonius, Primus, and the famous Dionysius of Corinth (170 A.D.), who wrote letters to the Lacedaemonians, Athenians, Nicomedians, as well as to the church of Gortyna and the other Cretan dioceses, to the churches in Pontus, and Rome, exhorting them not to fall into heresy and schism. In his letter to the Romans, Dionysius of Corinth wrote that St. Paul and St. Peter both preached the gospel in Corinth. "For both Peter and Paul, having planted us at Corinth, likewise instructed us; and having in a like manner taught in Italy, they suffered martyrdom about the same time." At the First Ecumenical Council of Nicaea in 325 A.D., the Corinthian church was represented by its bishop Epikletus.

RHODES

We know very little about St. Paul's activities on his third missionary journey, to which St. Luke devotes only a few lines.

> Paul sent for the disciples and having exhorted them took leave of them and departed for Macedonia. When he had gone through these parts and had given them much encouragement, he came to Greece. There he spent three months, and when a plot was made against him by the Jews as he was about to sail for Syria, he determined to return through Macedonia.
>
> Acts 20:1-3

There is, however, a good deal of information about St. Paul's return voyage from Greece to Jerusalem, some episodes of which are recorded in the Acts and others are accepted as tradition. Traveling north from Corinth, St. Paul revisited the brethren in Philippi, the center of his missionary activity in Macedonia, where he stayed for the Feast of the Unleavened Bread. With St. Luke and the elders of the churches of Veria, Thessalonica, and Derbe he went to Neapolis and sailed for Troy. The crossing took five days, presumably because of unfavorable winds. The Apostle stayed seven days in Troy, and during one of his lengthy sermons a young man named Eutychus fell asleep while sitting on the window sill and fell three floors to the ground. The young man was picked up from the ground as dead but when the Apostle came down to him he held him gently in his arms and assured those present that Eutychus was alive and would recover (Acts 20:7-12).

St. Luke and the elders embarked from Troy, but St. Paul went by land to the small port of Assos on the southern coast of the Troad and there joined his companions on board ship. They traveled via Mytilene, Chios, and Samos to Miletus on the west coast of Asia Minor, where St. Paul delivered his touching farewell address to the elders of Ephesus (Acts 20:17-35).

With a favorable wind the ship sailed on to Cos, famous for its Sanctuary of Asklepios. St. Luke, the Christian physician, who was well acquainted with the eastern Mediterranean, would not have been ignorant of the religious and medical fame of Cos. With gratitude he would have reflected, as the ship lay at anchor near the city of Hippocrates, that he had been freed from the bonds of superstition.

The following day they sailed passed Cape Triopium and the peninsula of Cnidus and landed at the capital of the island of Rhodes. As the ship sailed into the harbor of Rhodes, St. Paul would have seen the remains of the Colossus, one of the Seven Wonders of the ancient world. This impressive bronze monument was built between 304 and 284 B.C., but collapsed during an earthquake in 225 B.C. Its height was between 90 and 120 feet and its weight close to 250 tons. According to Strabo the Colossus was broken at the knees and, because of an oracle, the people of Rhodes did not attempt to raise it again. Unfortunately, we have no archaeological evidence concerning the former location of the Colossus, although a Rhodian tradition asserts that the Colossus stood on the site of the Gate of St. Paul. Its remains were sold in 656 A.D. by Mu'awiyah, the first 'Umayyad caliph, to a Jewish merchant of Emesa, Syria, who used 900 camels to cart the pieces away.

The Rhodians maintain that the Apostle stayed in their city and preached, bringing many people into the new faith. Before he left, we are told, St. Paul appointed Prochorus, one of the seven deacons (Acts 6:5), bishop of the island. Prochorus was succeeded by Ephranoras and then by Photinas.

Another local tradition, held in Lindos on the southeast coast of the island, has the Apostle's ship arrive at the island in the small harbor at the foot of the acropolis of Lindos, where pilgrims for centuries had worshiped Athena Lindia. To this day the small harbor is referred to as "St. Paul's Harbor" and a small barrel-

Rhodes: St. Paul's Gate

Rhodes: St. Paul's Bay, Lindos

Anthony Pachos

vaulted chapel of St. Paul commemorates the landing and preaching of the Apostle.

What St. Dionysius the Areopagite is for Athens, St. Titus for Crete, St. Barnabas for Cyprus, and St. Demetrius for Thessalonica, St. Silas, a prophet and leader among the brethren (Acts 15:22-23), is for Rhodes. The Rhodians tell how St. Silas had visited several villages on the island but his message had been questioned by the villagers of Sorone, twenty miles to the southwest of the capital. St. Silas proved the power of Jesus Christ by healing a paralytic, whereupon the villagers accepted the Christian faith and built a church in honor of their patron.

Cos: The Sanctuary of Asklepios

CRETE

The Apostle's last visit to Greece was accidental. After his return to Jerusalem at the end of his third missionary journey St. Paul was accused of taking a Gentile Ephesian into the inner court of the Temple, thereby desecrating the holy of holies. The Apostle would almost certainly have been killed had not the commander of the Antonia fortress on the edge of the temple area protected him from the angry mob. The account of St. Paul's arrest, imprisonment, and appearances before several tribunals spreads over many verses and occupies a disproportionate amount of space in the Acts of the Apostles. It appears almost as if St. Luke were trying to compare the passion of his hero with the passion of our Lord. In this context, G.H.C. Macgregor has written that

> like Jesus, Paul appears before the Sanhedrin, is handed over by his fellow countrymen to the Gentiles, is accused before a Roman governor, and the charge again culminates in an accusation of treason against Caesar. This resemblance is not due to arbitrary invention. It is the natural working out of a law which had been enunciated by the Lord himself: "as the master, so shall the servant be." At his trial before Porcius Festus at Caesarea, St. Paul appealed to Caesar (Acts 25:11), whereupon Festus, after conferring with his advisers, replied to the Apostle: "You have appealed to Caesar, to Caesar you shall go."

St. Luke has preserved for us the story of St. Paul's last voyage, which took him from Jerusalem to Caesarea, Myra, Crete, Melita, Puteoli, and Rome. In many ways, this account is the most dramatic piece of writing in the Acts of the Apostles, largely because the author was an eyewitness to what he related.

Fair Havens
Source: Spratt, T.A.B., *Travels and Researches in Crete,* London, 1865

We sailed slowly for a number of days, and arrived with difficulty off Cnidus, and as the wind did not allow us to go on, we sailed under the lee of Crete off Salmone. Coasting along with difficulty, we came to a place called Fair Havens, near which was the city of Lasea. As much time had been lost, and the voyage was already dangerous because the fast had already gone by, Paul advised them saying, "Sirs, I perceive that the voyage will be with injury and much loss, not only of the cargo, and the ship, also of our lives." But the centurion paid more attention to the captain and to the owner of the ship than to what Paul said. And because the harbor was not suitable to winter in, the majority advised to put to sea from there, on the chance that somehow they could reach Phoenix, a harbor of Crete, looking northeast and southeast, and winter there. And when the south wind blew gently, supposing that they had obtained their purpose, they weighed anchor and sailed along Crete, close inshore. But soon a tempestuous wind, called the northeaster, struck down from the land; and when the ship was caught and could not face the wind, we gave way to it and were driven.   Acts 27:7-15

Some scholars maintain that St. Paul's departure from Caesarea should be placed towards the end of August 61. According to Acts 27:5 in the Western Text, the voyage from Caesarea to Myra took fifteen days. Considering the slow progress because of unfavorable weather conditions, the ship carrying the Apostle anchored at Fair Havens near Lasea about the end of the first week of October 61. Here the ship stayed for some time, waiting for the wind to change.

We do not know exactly how long the ship anchored at Fair Havens, although it has been suggested that their stay lasted about three weeks prior to the meeting between St. Paul, the centurion, the captain, and the owner, and perhaps even a few days after the meeting while waiting for a favorable wind.

Fair Havens, known in Greek as Kaloi Limenes or Kalous Limionas, is the name of a small village, a bay, and a group of islets about five and a half miles west of Cape Leon on the

Crete: The Bay of Loutro (Phoenix)

Justin Lee

southern coast of Crete. The 18th century English traveler
Richard Pococke only heard of it when he happened to be in the
area, and the early 19th century traveler Robert Pashley, who
otherwise has told us so much about Crete, only looked down
on it while passing over the neighboring hills. The first modern
description of this biblical site comes from the pen of Captain
T.A.B. Spratt, who commanded the paddle steamer "Spitfire"
through the waters off the southern coast of Crete. In 1851
Captain Spratt anchored where, a little more than eighteen
hundred years before, St. Paul's ship had sought shelter. New
Testament in hand, Spratt went ashore.

> Upon the dark slaty ridge rising immediately over the
> western bay forming the haven, we unexpectedly found the
> ruins of a Greek chapel, still dedicated to St. Paul, perhaps
> marking the very spot where the Apostle himself used to
> preach to the natives of Crete when the Gospel was first

planted there by him during the ship's stay. A small part of the site of the old church, enclosed by four low walls of loose stones, and therefore entirely open to the heavens, is still used by the natives as a chapel.

Nearby they found fragments of marble as well as the foundations of walls which may have belonged to an older church.

The existing white chapel, commemorating the Apostle's arrival on Crete, is situated on the brow of the hill overlooking the bay. It is built upon the site of the former church. A few yards to the west of the church is the traditional cave, marked by a tall cross where the Apostle stayed. The few houses of Kaloi Limenes are scattered around the bay. A bunker station with several oil tanks was recently built on the largest island of this picturesque bay.

In addition to Kaloi Limenes, some Cretans maintained that the Apostle preached at Hierapetra. Between 1671 and 1679 Bernard Randolph visited a cave about ten miles east of Hierapetra.

> It is a large chappel having twelve pillars cut out of the rock, which was done by the Christians at night time. Close by is a fountain where they say he used to baptize, and is now called St. Paul's Fountain, the water thereof is very good, to cure such as have sore eyes.

During his stay in Kaloi Limenes St. Paul met the owner and the captain of the ship, and advised them of the danger of continuing the journey. He had every reason to warn them for he was speaking from personal experience. Three times he had been shipwrecked, and at least once he had spent twenty-four hours in the open sea (II Cor. 11:25). The officers of the ship, however, decided otherwise and the centurion accepted their advice.

Crete: The cave and chapel of St. Paul at Kaloi Limenes

Crete: The Church of St. Paul between Loutro and Aghia Roumeli

Marc Dubin

Phoenix, now known as Loutro, several miles to the west, was a far better harbor for waiting out the winter. The people of Loutro maintain that the Apostle visited their town either on this or a later journey. Several travelers have pointed out the little chapel of St. Paul and the spring named after him between Loutro and Aghia Roumeli on the southern coast of Crete. The chapel is best reached by boat. It is first mentioned by the 15th century Florentine traveler Buondelmonti, who also speaks of this spring as being half the size of his own Arno, which must have been an extravagant exaggeration. Robert Pashley visited the chapel in 1834 and referred to a "plenteous spring of fresh water rushing out of the beach and flowing for a few paces before it loses itself in the sea." Today the only sign that remains of this once important spring is the water that bubbles up through some pebbles at the very edge of the sea. The chapel, once adorned with beautiful wall paintings which have since been lost, stands all by itself, like, as Professor Dawkins has written, "a valuable casket accidentally dropped on the shore."

Justin Lee

The chapel commemorates the site where St. Paul is supposed to have baptized his first Cretan converts. A service is held in the chapel each year, on the feasts of SS. Peter and Paul (June 29).

The ship left Fair Havens with favorable wind, but as soon as they reached the open sea they fell victim to a strong northeast wind. Only the residents of the Levant can fully appreciate this statement, for these annual late summer storms, known in Greece as the meltemi, cause a great deal of damage and discomfort. The term meltemi probably derives from the Italian bel tempo, because it occurs only in the summer. It is a north northwesterly to north northeasterly gale. Undoubtedly, it was this storm in which the Apostle's ship was caught.

According to Cretan tradition, St. Paul visited the island on another occasion apart from the few days when the ship in which he was being taken to Rome was blown to Fair Havens. Neither the circumstances nor the short time he was in Crete on that occasion could have given him the opportunity to travel and

111

Herakleion: Cathedral of St. Titus

preach and acquire the wide knowledge and experience of the place and its people which are reflected in the *Epistle to Titus*. It is therefore thought that when the Apostle was released from his first imprisonment in Rome in 64 A.D., he started a fourth missionary journey in the course of which he preached at Gortyna, the island's capital, and established the Christian church on Crete commissioning Titus to complete the work. In Gortyna, the capital of Crete during the Roman period, are the ruins of the church of St. Titus, which date from the 4th century. Tradition holds that St. Paul appointed Titus bishop of the island on the site of this church.

The whole issue of St. Paul's mission to the island depends of course upon the authenticity of the Pauline authorship of the Pastoral Epistles in general, and the one written to Titus in particular. The remark "this is why I left you in Crete, that you might amend what was defective, and appoint elders in every town as I directed you" (Titus 1:5) suggests that the author of this epistle had labored there for some time. And yet beyond this statement nothing else is reported of such a mission either in the canonical or apocryphal literature as, for example, in the Acts of Paul. Modern New Testament scholarship is sharply divided on the issue of the Pauline authorship of this epistle. For us it is sufficient to note that the Gospel was introduced to Crete by Cretan Jews, who were among those who received the Holy Spirit in Jerusalem on the first Pentecost (Acts 2:1), and who would have returned to their native island following the annual festivities.

The people of Crete entertain a number of traditions about the Apostle's missionary activities on their island. One of these is that he banished poisonous snakes from Crete. When Robert Pashley visited the island in 1834 he was told that, after his residence in Rome, St. Paul returned to Crete where he freed the inhabitants from "wild beasts and noxious animals." Less than twenty years later Captain Spratt encountered a lay brother from a nearby monastery who told him a similar tale,

> that while lighting a fire on the shore, the Apostle Paul was bitten by a serpent, but it did him no harm, although very venomous. From that time all the snakes in Crete were charmed by St. Paul and became harmless.

Diodorus of Sicily (60 B.C.) held Herakles responsible for achieving this deed, and Plutarch used this information as a point of comparison when he stated that "it may be possible to find a country in which, as it is recorded of Crete, there are no wild animals, but a government which has not had to bear with envy and jealous rivalry or contention has not hitherto existed." Reportedly, there are no venomous snakes on Crete. There are two kinds of snakes: one is called *ophes,* which is smaller and, as some believe, is the sort of viper which fastened on St. Paul's hand in Melita (Acts 28: 3-6). Whether this Cretan tradition is a mere transfer of the same story that is still being told in Melita (present-day Malta) or whether it developed in fulfillment of the promise by Jesus Christ, "Behold, I have given you authority to

Gortyna: Shrine of St. Titus in the ruined Church of St. Titus

tread upon serpents and scorpions... and nothing shall hurt you" (Luke 10:19) is, of course, difficult to know.

One of the numerous arguments advanced against the Pauline authorship of the *Epistle to Titus* is the remark about the character of the Cretans.

> For there are many insubordinate men, empty talkers and deceivers, especially the circumcision party; they must be silenced, since they are upsetting whole families by teaching for base gain what they have no right to teach. One of themselves, a prophet of their own, said, "Cretans are always liars, evil beasts, lazy gluttons." This testimony is true. Therefore rebuke them sharply. . . .
>
> Titus 1:10-13

Such a remark by the Apostle would have been singularly untactful, and yet the Cretans have lived with this and even worse criticisms of their collective character for many centuries. The quotation about the Cretans being "always liars, evil beasts and lazy gluttons" is attributed to the 6th century B.C. poet Epimenides of Knossos who, in spite of this statement, was honored by the Cretans as a god to whom sacrifices were offered. Epimenides had called the Cretans liars because they claimed to possess the tomb of Zeus, whereas his devotees maintained that he was not dead.

Some Cretans seem to have accepted the apostolic judgment. Captain Spratt mentions that with respect to the Biblical statement "This witness is true" there seems

> to have been a community that responded to it as being true, for there is, strangely, if not appropriately, a village opposite Gortyna called "Truth" or "The Truthful," Aletheia or Alethiana being its name, which is thus echoed from the very hills that face the city.

But other Cretans maintain a tradition according to which St. Paul was beaten up by a busybody and barely escaped with his life because of the remarks which are recorded in the Epistle to Titus.

Herakleion: Icon of St. Paul on the iconostasis of the Cathedral of St. Titus

After leaving Crete, the ship carrying the Apostle only just succeeded in reaching Melita where he and his companions remained for three months, resuming their journey in March of the following year. In April 62 St. Paul entered Rome. The narrative in the Acts of the Apostles concludes by saying that St. Paul remained in Rome for two full years in his own rented apartment, welcoming all who came to see him, preaching the Kingdom of God and teaching about the Lord Jesus Christ openly and unhindered (Acts 28:30-31).

BIBLIOGRAPHY

Babin, J.P., *Relation de l'état présent de la ville d'Athènes*, Lyon, 1674.

Bire, Costas E., ῾Ο ᾽Απόστολος Παῦλος ἐν ᾽Αθήναις, Athens, 1962.

Bornkamm, Günther, *Paulus*, Stuttgart, 1969.

Brassac, A., "Une inscription de Delphes et la chronologie de Saint Paul" *Revue Biblique*. N.S.X., 1913, pp. 36-53, 207-217.

Bratsiotis, P.I. (ed.), *Paulus-Hellas-Oikumene. An Ecumenical Symposium. 1900th Anniversary of the Coming of St. Paul to Greece*, Athens, 1951.

Broneer, Oscar, "Corinth, Center of St. Paul's Missionary Work in Greece." *The Biblical Archaeologist*, XIV, 4, 1951, pp. 78-96.

"The Apostle Paul and the Isthmian Games." *The Biblical Archaeologist*, XXV, 1962, 1, pp. 2-31.

"Studies in Topography of Corinth in the Time of St. Paul." ᾽Αρχαιολογικὴ ᾽Εφημερὶς, 1937, pp. 125-133.

Cadbury, Henry J., *The Making of Luke-Acts*, New York, 1927.

Chandler, Richard, *Travels in Asia Minor and Greece*, London, 1817.

Chatzidadkis, Manolis, *Byzantine Athens*, Athens, n.d.

Conybeare, W.J. and Howson, J.S., *The Life and Epistles of St. Paul*, Vol. I, London, 1863.

Craig, C.T., "The First Epistle to the Corinthians," *The Interpreter's Bible*, vol. X, New York, 1953.

De Dreux, Robert, *Voyage en Turquie et en Grèce*, Paris, 1925.

De La Guillatière, *An Account of a Late Voyage to Athens, Containing the Estate Both Ancient and Modern of that Famous City*, London, 1676.

Dinkler, Erich, "Das Bema zu Korinth", *Marburger Jahrbuch für Kunstwissenschaft*, XIII, pp. 12-22.

Elderkin, George W., "Golgotha, Kraneion and the Holy Sepulchre." *Archaeological Papers*, VII, Springfield, 1945.

Feavers, D., "Corinth at the Time of St. Paul." *Papers of the American School of Classical Studies in Athens*, 1952.

Finegan, Paul, *Light from the Ancient Past,* Princeton, 1946, pp. 269-271.

Frazer, J.G., *Pausanias's Description of Greece,* London, 1913.

Goodenough, Erwin R., *Jewish Symbols in the Graeco-Roman Period,* New York, 1953.

Goodspeed, Edgar J., *An Introduction to the New Testament,* Chicago, 1937.

Gritsopoulos, T.A., "Ἐκκλησιαστικὴ Ἱστορία Κορινθίας." Πελοποννισιακά, 1972.

Harnack, Adolf von, *The Acts of the Apostles,* tr. J.R. Wilkinson, London, 1909.

Hawthorne, John G., "Cenchreae Port of Corinth," *Archaeology,* XVIII, 1965, pp. 191-200.

Hobhouse, J.C., *A Journey through Albania and Other Provinces of Turkey,* London, 1815.

Kinsey, Robert S., *With Paul in Greece,* Nashville, Tenn., 1957.

Leake, William Martin, *Travels in Northern Greece,* London, 1835.

Lehmann-Hartleben, "Die antiken Hafenanlagen." *Klio Beiheft,* XIV, 1923, pp. 148-152.

Macgregor, G.H.C., "The Acts of the Apostles," *The Interpreter's Bible,* Vol. IX, New York, 1954.

Mattill, A. J. and M. B., *A Classified Bibliography of Literature on the Acts of the Apostles.* (6646 entries of books and articles), Leiden, 1966.

McDonald, W.A., "Archaeology and St. Paul's Journeys in Greek Lands," *The Biblical Archaeologist,* III, 2, 1940, pp. 18-24; IV, 1, 1941, pp. 1-10; V, 3, 1942, pp. 36-48.

Meinardus, O.F.A., "An Athenian Tradition: St. Paul's Refuge in the Well," *Ostkirchliche Studien* XXI, 1972, pp. 181-186.

Meyer, Eduard, *Ursprung und Anfänge des Christentums,* Stuttgart, 1921.

Metzger, Bruce M., *Index to Periodical Literature on the Apostle Paul,* Leiden, 1960.

Metzger, Henri, *Les Routes de Saint Paul dans l'Orient Grec,* Neuchâtel, 1954.

Morton, H. V., *In the Steps of St Paul,* London, 1963.

Ogg, George, *The Odyssey of Paul. A Chronology*, New Jersey, 1968.

Parente, P. P., "St. Paul's Address before the Areopagus" *Catholic Biblical Quarterly*, (Washington), XI, 1949, pp. 144-150.

Pashley, Robert, *Travels in Crete*, London, 1837.

Pelekides, St., Περὶ μιᾶς στήλης, *Πεπραγμένα τοῦ (·) Διεθνοῦς Βυζαντινολογικοῦ Συνεδρίου*, I, Thessalonica, 1953, p. 408.

Perlzweig, Judith, *Lamps from the Athenian Agora*, Princeton, 1963.

Ramsay, William Mitchell, *St. Paul the Traveller and the Roman Citizen*, London, 1927.

Scranton, R.L. "The Corinth of the Apostle Paul." *The Emory University Quarterly*, V, 2, 1949.

Scranton, R.L., and Ramage, E.S., "Investigations at Kenchreai." *Hesperia*, XXXIII, 1963, pp. 134-145.

Shear, Leslie T., "The Athenian Agora: Excavations of 1970" *Hesperia*, XL, 1971, pp. 241-260.

Smith, James, *The Voyage and Shipwreck of St. Paul*, London, 1880.

Smith, Michael Lewellyn, *The Great Island; a study of Crete*, London, 1965.

Spratt, T. A. B., *Travels and Researches in Crete*, London, 1865.

Streeter, B. H., *The Primitive Church*, New York, 1929.

Sukenik, E., *Ancient Synagogues in Palestine and Greece*, London, 1934.

Vanderpool, Eugene, "The Apostle Paul in Athens," *Archaeology*. III, I, 1950, pp. 34-37.

Weiss, Johannes, *The History of Primitive Christianity*, ed. F. C. Grant, New York, 1937.

INDEX

123

125

Other Lycabettus Press Publications

Athens-Auschwitz, by Errikos Sevillias
Christians in the Arab East, by Robert B. Betts
Cookbook of the Jews of Greece, by Nicholas Stavroulakis
Delphi, by Alan Walker
Doorway to Greece, by Mary Winterer-Papatassos
Epidaurus (Greek), by Nikolaos Faraklas
Greek Assignments, SOE 1943 - 1948 UNSCOB, by Michael Ward
Greek Calendar Cookbook, by Anne Yannoulis
Greek Dances, by Ted Petrides
Kos, by Chris and Christa Mee
Lefkadia (English and Greek editions), by J. Touratzoglou
Nauplion, by Timothy E. Gregory
Naxos, by John Freely
Paros (German), by Jeffrey Carson and James Clark
Paros, Roads, Trails, and Beaches,
    by Jeffrey Carson and James Clark
Patmos, by Tom Stone
Poros, by Niki Stavrolakes
St. John of Patmos and the Seven Churches of the Apocalypse,
    by Otto F. A. Meinardus
St. Paul in Ephesus and the Cities of Galatia and Cyprus,
    by Otto F. A. Meinardus
The Jews of Ioannina, by Rae Dalven
The Other Side of the Road (for children, English and Greek
    editions), by Elizabeth Boleman Herring
The Unwritten Places, by Tim Salmon
Tom Stone's Greek Food and Drink Book, by Tom Stone
Tom Stone's Greek Handbook, by Tom Stone
Vergina (English and Greek editions), by M. Andronicos